Through The Light Of

Sola Scriptura

Prescription For Everlasting Life

An Essential Guide to Identify the True Christian Congregation and Help Every Believer to Engage Steadfastly on the Road to Eternity.

Jean Daniel François, M.D.

Other Books Of The Same Author

Keys to Authentic Success (in French)

Prescription For A Successful Life

Prescription For A Successful Career in Medicine

Prescription For An Exciting Love Life

The No Nonsense Approach To A Successful Life

You may visit the author's web site: www.successfullife.us,

Or you may e-mail to jfranc6704@gmail.com

Jean Daniel François, MD
c/o G.O.A.L, Inc.
1713-19 Ralph Avenue
Brooklyn, NY 11236
Phone: 718-531-6100, Fax 718-531-2329

Table of Contents

The Scripture quotations are from the Holy Bible written by various authors, but primarily the King James Version.

Printed in USA
First Edition

Cover designed and prepared by Denise Gibson
ISBN: 978-0-9823142-5-8

For any information, write:
Jean Daniel François, MD
P. O. Box 360543
Brooklyn, NY 11236 USA

Phone (718) 531-6100, Fax (718) 531-2329
E-mail: jfranc6704@gmail.com

www.successfullife.us

For my mother,

For Uncle Garcia,

In memory of my godmother and Aunt Rosette whose remains have disappeared after the earthquake of January 12, 2010,

In memory of my father,

For my family, all my friends,

and all those who persevere in faith.

aveat

This task began innocently in early summer 2009 when I quickly had to come up with a sermon to compensate for the absence of a pastor at my church. I ran into the second chapter of Acts of the Apostles. I was really fascinated. It was as if I had just discovered a gold ore. Strangely enough, it is a passage with which I am very familiar. Its impact on me was so strong, that evening I decided to reserve it and elaborate on it for another occasion. That exercise led to what you have in your hand. Many could find the title daring and complex. In the 21st century, priority often is given to people with pompous titles, those who are highly qualified as experts and who are recognized worldwide. They set the tone and whatever they say goes. But if truth was solely dependent upon diplomas, academic performances and ranking, the outstanding men in Jesus' time would have known the signs and identified Jesus as the Son of God while he was among them. Unfortunately, because of prejudice, they did not. They even crucified Him. According to MATTHEW 11:25, Jesus stated that divine truth is hidden from the wise and the intelligent of this world, yet it is revealed to children. Here, 'children' means those who are humble, simple and ready to act in good faith. We can spend our lives arguing, philosophizing, speculating, extrapolating and making inferences, yet nothing can change the TRUTH that most people tend to reject in favor of reasoning that fits with their way of life and is based on false premises. No need to be among the best scholars to realize that our world is heading towards the abyss while still searching for the TRUTH. So many voices claim to have found it by presenting various forms of philosophies, theories, theologies, religions and doctrines, and many have become confused, skeptical, and others have given up all together. This is in the midst of such a 'hurly burly' that I dare to submit to you, dear reader, a simple and practical approach in your quest to find the TRUTH, to identify the true Christian and the authentic church. According to ECCLESIASTES 12:13, *"Let us hear the conclusion of the whole matter: Fear God, and keep His Commandments: for this is the whole duty of man."*

Note to Readers.

Because some of you may not be too familiar with the Bible, let me quickly state that it is a compilation of 66 books written by various authors, but all under the Holy Spirit's influence. Generally, it is comprised of two parts: the Old and The New Testaments. When a text is cited, it is important to realize in which Testament, which book, chapter, then verse to find if. For example, JOHN 3:16 represents the book of John (in the New Testament), chapter 3 and verse 16. To make it easier, to find out about a given text in a given book in the Bible, please refer to the Table of Contents of your Bible, where you will see where a particular book is found. Thanks!

cknowledgements

Several people have seen these pages and I appreciate their criticism and advice. Once again I extend a special thanks to all of those who are always willing to give me much needed advice. I thank God for your help. Special thanks to Ms Diana Rivers, Ms Martine Michel and Ms Rashidah J. Suleiman who spent precious time reviewing the manuscript.

I am very grateful to them and many others, including engineer/author Ernst St. Louis. I am also grateful to Ms Denise Gibson who goes out of her way to guide me in any way possible and get me a cover that finally satisfies me. I cannot specifically thank all those who helped me, but, please accept my sincere thanks to all of you.

~ JEAN DANIEL FRANÇOIS

"I am a fellow citizen of every soul who thinks: the truth is my country."

Alphonse de Lamartine

(translation from French)

Address and Greeting

Dear friends:

I write to you dear pastors because you have custody of the flock of God.

I write to you dear leaders because your influence and your teaching largely determine the ultimate fate of believers.

I write to you dear parents because you are the first direct representatives of God toward your children.

I write to you educators because you are molding young minds one way or another.

I write to you dear young people because you have the key to the destiny of the world. If you have no compass, the world will follow you to the precipice.

I write to you dear children, because the Master has always given you a princely place in his ministry.

I write to you dear brethren because you are the guardian of the priesthood in the home.

I write to you dear sisters as children learn the first notions of value at your knees.

I write to you all, because, like the apostle John, I love you all and I hope that each one of you makes an informed choice regarding his or her ultimate destiny.

Sincerely,

Jean Daniel François

Introduction

Since the genesis of humanity, everything has revolved around the constant desire to pursue happiness as the *summum bonum* (ultimate good). The fleeting shadow of this bliss puts man into constant motion, like a dog chasing its tail it never catches. Then comes the twilight of his life, when he is crestfallen and breathless, and forced to admit he has not had a better fate than his elders. He, too, has not discovered this unique and precious pearl that remains the universal search and the generative principle of human existence. Exhausted, he consoles himself by listing his accomplishments, his scientific prowess, his financial prosperity, his great intellectual capacity, his popularity, or his comfort.

Even at the beginning of this new century, despite all the discoveries, the supreme urge and search for happiness remains but an illusion. Moreover, it seems that life has become even more difficult. The people of the world are unanimous in recognizing that we live in an era of worrisome human existence. One crisis follows another, and conflicts abound. Everywhere it is anxiety, anguish, or despair. Everyone is eager to discover a magic solution that solves it all. This remains elusive. Among the methods tested to capture what seems unattainable, some people embrace religion to probe the fundamental mystery of life. But again the diversity of opinions is growing. What is religion? Is one religion superior to another? What should its role in the life of mankind be? Does religion define man or does man define religion? This has been controversial throughout history. As a matter of fact, contrary to the intent of the founders of different faiths, it is unfortunate — even shameful — to admit the amount of pain and suffering caused by religion throughout history. Often religion has been at the heart of many conflicts. This is one of the strongest ties that bind or divide men. According to the World Christian Encyclopedia, there are approximately 10,000 religions on this earth. Christianity, Judaism and Islam, the pillars of the Abrahamic monotheism, disagree among themselves. Even in the Christian world, differences persist. Otherwise, we would not have more than 33,000 different variations under the umbrella of Christianity. This facilitates a flow of cynicism from some and skepticism from others. The big question is and remains, how can man find happiness? Where do we find the truth? Often we are more interested in a concept than in the reality that it implies. We seek the absolute, but with preconceived ideas. Our assessment is polluted by our culture and values we have internalized. We read, see, act and interpret everything through the prism of our understanding and our training, which are contaminated with our emotions. The little individualistic bundle we are made of depends on what we have learned, inherited, seen, heard and understood. The interpretation of reality requires impartiality. Authentic TRUTH is inconvenient for most of us. It requires loyalty, honesty, and integrity to accept. The century in which we live does not lend itself to such scrutiny. Often we forget that man has become the measure of everything that exists. Everything that he touches is 'contaminated' by his weaknesses, temperament, prejudices, beliefs, level of intelligence and intellectual training, culture, habits, economic status, friends, race, dreams and ambitions. Very often man takes a stand for reasons that he cannot explain, and when his subconscious questions him for his action, or the result of his choice, he wonders, or even wants to retaliate. No one can identify the true motive behind every action, not even oneself. Alas. Here is the same vulnerable being, with all his shortcomings, whose ambition is to find and define TRUTH objectively. Once he defines it, he feels mandated to use all means to impose it. That is why there are fanatics in every religion. In the light of their evocative interpretation, many people not only want to twist the meaning of the word to be in harmony with their own life, but also they want to impose their 'truth' on others by any means, including threats, coercion, alienation, persecution, disposal or destruction. That said, you've probably already guessed my dilemma. When I dare to begin writing this book, I wanted to make sure that I put aside all preconceived ideas, pressures, and personal biases to let the sacred oracles do the talking. "Sola Scriptura!" I pledge solemnly with all my heart to silence any prejudice, ignore all caution, put my personal preferences aside, and to focus on what is TRUE regardless of the consequences. I sincerely desire to drain all transcendent truth. May Heaven grant me the courage and wisdom to put aside all my prejudices and not let my personal views show in these pages. Let the ax fall where it may. The truth shall triumph. My compass should be the Book of Books, the BIBLE, because it reveals the love, wisdom, power, faithfulness and mercy of Jehovah. It is the source that teaches about salvation, faith, and perfect behavior. It regulates the vertical relationships — human and divine, and the (interpersonal) horizontal relationship. The regular Kings James version will be used to avoid confusion. However, bear in mind any regular Bible can do the job. If any reader does not recognize the Bible as a reference book, then the challenge begins. Ultimately, it is worth reading this book, if only for your personal information or formation. Thank you!

orbidden To Free Thinkers

I respect everybody. Accordingly, I respect all those who fall into the category of 'free thinkers'. I see them as people devoid of any fanaticism, inspired in good faith, gifted with good judgment, and who adopt a balanced and impartial approach in order to analyze and interpret the data submitted to them so they can draw their own conclusions. The free thinkers are not embittered, obscurantist, activist or people filled with prejudice who automatically reject an idea because it is different from theirs. They know that any new approach or interpretation could, over time and analysis, project a glimmer of explanation to clarify the confused man or the eternal researcher who continues to question his origin and his *raison d'être* (reason for being). The concepts can be identical, but our explanations are different. That is why in all humility, I appeal to the reasoning / analytical mind, with discernment and patience of all thinkers, to read this book with an open mind.

A. The Role of Religion Through The Ages

Like it or not, religion has always played a major role in the dynamics of civilizations. Within societies and cultures, no one can ignore the impact of religious denominations. However, this concept is appreciated in different ways. Some welcome religion as the spearhead to fight against the structures of alienation, and promote recovery of the inalienable rights of all human beings. Others accuse it of being an effective tool to pacify the exploited and appease the conscience of the exploiters.

In this imbroglio, some people choose to be mere spectators as they face their own questions on different areas of life. Such an approach is considered prudent and wise by this century's standards. However, there are certain areas where silence and indifference become a deafening vote to support one position or another. You need to remain consistent with yourself, be aware that your future depends on past and present choices and actions. No one can sit idly by because all of us have to face the final outcome of our lives or our final destiny. To facilitate this time of reflection, let us walk together in that delicate, yet mysterious journey.

B. The Concept of God, Philosophical or Scientific Concept?

What do we know about the concept of God? Frankly, no one can claim to never have heard of religion or ever thought of the concept of eternity. Many would like to be the 'Investigator of the Most High'. Even those who boast of being independent, 'strong-minded beings' need to admit that somehow, there comes a point where even his prodigious intelligence leads him to question his own certainties about the end of earthly life issues. After all, thinking, questioning, and even doubting can lead to great discoveries. Some circumstances can torpedo fundamental beliefs. Even if only by pure reflex, for a few brief seconds, the notion of the role of God touches everyone's thoughts.

Let us approach it with simplicity, sincerity, and patience with our heads above our shoulders. Let us be sensible enough to look around us and reflect on the essence of life, its origin, purpose and ultimate outcome. By doing so, it will be difficult to resist thinking of this concept of divinity that has captivated the attention of men throughout time. Whether you are a philosopher, theologian, religious idealist, poet, metaphysician, scientist or politician, just like ordinary mortals, you cannot resist the desire to give or have an opinion about EL SHADDAI. From Socrates to Nietzsche, from Plato to Heidegger through St. Augustine, St. Thomas Aquinas, and Descartes, everybody tries to argue for or against Yahweh, or attempts to reconcile faith with reason. Why? Because the human race is made up of cultural beings. Even those involved in science and neuroscience are beginning to discuss the issue of man being wired with a spiritual connection.

C. Could a Gene Be Responsible For The Trend of Worship In Human?

In fact according to some researchers, including psychologist Laura Koenig and molecular biologist Dean H. Hammer, there seems to be a genetic bent toward spirituality, the so-called 'God gene': VMAT2. According to *The God Gene: How Faith Is Hardwired Into Our Genes*, by geneticist Dean H. Hammer, there is a place in the brain with a genetic predisposition to worship. This spiritual gene 'VMAT2' encodes a protein that helps transport monoamines. VMAT2 plays an important role in the availability of neurotransmitters in the brain including dopamine and serotonin. Of course several factors have contributed to the spirituality of individuals, including heritability, culture, civilization, economics, age, education, logic and the environment. We cannot say a single gene determines our spirituality. We must at least acknowledge that several genes play a role in our tendency to believe in something or someone. Our faith and our choices can atrophy or develop based on our actions and our attitudes. The history of man's tendency to worship goes back to time immemorial. We need at least to recognize that it is not only the effect of chance.

D. What If God Himself Had Planned and Wanted It?

Some cannot resist the idea to ask; *is it possible that The Creator has reserved a small corner in the human's brain to bring it to consider the possibility of the influence of God in his life?* It is often said that any work of value immediately raises the question: who created it. Indeed, marveling at a beautiful work of art, listening to a musical selection, or reading a poem, or a specially well written book, we hear the refrain: Who composed it? Who wrote it? When we identify a work of genius, we accept it and its author with open arms, even if some prejudices have caused doubt on the part of some spectators. We may want to try to assign someone's work to several other people that we deem to be better qualified for such great achievement. We can imagine all kinds of explanations to reject the authenticity of the work, or cast doubt on its creator. Sooner or later, we end up accepting the work and its author, if only out of respect of the 'copyright'.

When we contemplate the heavens, the moon and the stars, we see beauty, harmony, and power. Nature is majestic, creation is beautifully organized, and nothing is left to chance. Who is not fascinated by the elements of nature: thousands of fragrances in the gardens, a flower that a human tear drop has hatched, the first flight of a butterfly, the changing of the seasons, the tack of the rivers, giant trees at the mercy of the winds while silently recording everything that happens under their branches, the bright spring sun that rises to drive away the cold winter of the previous night and rekindle human's life, the moon sitting among the stars, shining like diamonds, the free birds that fly above meadows, the vast blue ocean that never sleeps, the majestic mountains that seem to touch the sky, the chirping birds, the routine animal songs, the reptiles, sea fish, insects! The pleasure felt while contemplating nature's wonders is indescribable. Isn't this lovely? Can we imagine the splendor of such beauty in the genesis of mankind?

When man came into existence, he found that everything was already done. As an intelligent being, there were questions and different views and assumptions. The answers depend on the source of faith and beliefs.

E. The Reconciliation of The Human and The Divine

The Bible says that Jehovah created everything. Christians accept that all things stem from the everlasting power and the divinity of the Creator. According to the Bible, Elohim was the authentic author. Genesis 1:27 says *"God created man in his own image, in the image of God created he him; male and female created he them."* Psalms 95:6 *"O come, let us worship and bow down; let us kneel before the Lord our maker."* Isaiah 45:12 *"I have made the earth, and created man upon it: I, even my hands, have stretched out the heavens, and all their host have I commanded."* But many are using their freedom of thought, intelligence and their God-given right to question, doubt and even refuse to accept what is said about the Almighty. They advance other theories and reject that which establishes God as the Author of all. But El Shaddai will not prosecute them.

F. Evolution Versus Creation

The theory of evolution speaks indirectly to herald a beginning by the 'Big Bang' The Bible also speaks of the genesis of our planet and everything in it, but it gives a different explanation: *"In the beginning God created..."* (Genesis 1:1).

G. The Bible Supports The Creation

The Bible, said in Psalms 19:1 *"The heavens declare the glory of God and the firmament sheweth his handy work."* Scientists are asked, why didn't the chaos last? What prompted it to organize? What has prevented another chaos to organize into something else since our existence?

In response, scientists explain all by the interaction of forces of physics. The union of these electric and magnetic forces, interacted with other physical forces and caused what we see. Where were these forces? Scientists admit that they have remained the same since the Big Bang; there has been no further transformation. They are vague about their origins. Why is it that since the existence of man we have not seen another chaotic condition turn into another series of events? How come man has never seen other bacteria, protozoa, or monkeys, evolve to create another creature like us? Did the Big Bang give rise to man and woman together, or was it the man who evolved into woman or vice versa? We imagine it will take a few more billions of years to get more explanations and hypotheses. The Bible says in

Genesis 1:2 that *"...the earth was without form, and void; and darkness was upon the face of the deep. And the Spirit of God moved upon the face of the waters."* Then God ordered by his words the creation of the world. The Bible also tells us in Genesis 2:21 that God created Adam, then He created Eve out of one of Adam's ribs. Instead of finding this approach too simplistic, why not marvel at a Creator so powerful? In Psalms 33:9 we read, *"For the LORD spake, and it was done; he commanded, and it stood fast."*

Common point between science and the divine: They obey laws.

Scientists admit that the universe contains forces that require legislation. Everything in the universe obeys to some kind of laws. Scientific discoveries also are subject to laws such as: physics, biology, chemistry, and thermodynamics, but a law is not promulgated spontaneously by itself. Every law requires a legislator or at least a hierarchy where the powerful triggers a chain of actions and reactions, dominates, or imposes their will. The order in the universe remains a fact. What is the cause? The existence of the universe requires at least a plausible contingency. The universe operates according to at least one principle. Therefore, the universe has a cause. We have to identify a reason or attribute it to a source.

First Conclusions.

Let us review the scientific approach that makes people reject the Almighty.

1. Scientists say there was a beginning stemming from a Big Bang. The Bible says in Genesis 1:1, *"In the beginning God created ..."* In other words, according to the Bible, not only was there a beginning, but it was determined, and organized by an eternal God with neither a beginning nor an end.

2. Scientists believe in their theories and make assumptions and deductions they have never seen, so they have faith in their theories based on observation and deduction.

Christians also have faith, but it is anchored on biblical truth. Is faith reasonable? Religion and reason go well together, but religion without reason, and based on imagination, and extremism, destroys and enslaves the mind, kidnaps all logic and leads to obscurantism, fanaticism and even ineptitude.

3. Scholars and the Bible both admit that man is a limited and mortal creature.

4. Scientists talk of a set of forces external to man, beyond man and all creation. This set of forces is omnipresent, immutable and perfect. Believers identify these forces as different manifestations of the Almighty Creator to whom everything is subject.

All in all, biblical knowledge with science should combine for greater and faster discoveries and progress on this planet.

The God of the universe: Supreme Being and indefinable.

We repeat the historical facts constantly, but we have no way to prove their absolute accuracy. Nevertheless, we believe them, and accept them. Historical events are not necessarily proven. A lot of reported events are accepted by faith. According to Napoleon Bonaparte, the truth of history probably will not be what has occurred, but only what will be told. According to famous American biologist Edwin Couklyn, trying to explain the early appearance of life by chance, is to admit that out of the explosion of a printing shop came a dictionary alone, by itself. One can even extrapolate and say it is like believing that following a chaotic explosion in an automobile plant, out came a Cadillac, a Mercedes or a Porsche.

Science cannot prove the existence or nonexistence of Yahweh. Why? Because He is immaterial. He does not operate according to man's parameters, or dimensions. His anatomical and physiological study, his DNA, and his fingerprint are not accessible to us. He cannot be felt, weighed, measured, placed somewhere or be subjected to the scientific study of man. When a finite, limited and visible being wants to understand an infinite, unlimited and multidimensional invisible God, this is pure madness. What is temporal cannot understand the timeless, the visible cannot identify the invisible. According to 1 Timothy 6:16, *"God only hath immortality, dwelling in the light which no man can approach unto; whom no man hath seen, nor can see; to whom be honor and power everlasting. Amen."*

All humans have an expiration date, death. Therefore, can we afford to spend our whole limited existence trying to comprehend, and **define the indefinable** in order to prove his existence?

In Ecclesiastes 1:13 Solomon says, *"I gave my heart to seek and search out by wisdom concerning all things that are done under heaven: it is a thankless occupation that God has given to the son of men, that they get tired."*

The Lord of Lords is beyond time and matter. His 'being' is not defined in terms of tangible and proven facts we want to impose. Any honest and informed mind must be unsatisfied with the answers that the great men, and impressive brains of the world have offered to these pertinent questions. If we cannot understand ourselves and our fellow men, how could we understand the Almighty?

The ultimate proof demanded by non-believers to explain or demonstrate the existence of God is impossible to give.

My grandmother used to tell the following story: a young man incredulously got up one day in the middle of a church service and challenged the pastor to prove the existence of God. The pastor, who was very familiar with the Bible, had no difficulty in citing verse after verse dealing with the existence and power of God. The incredulous young man was not impressed or satisfied after each verse. Finally, he told the pastor and the entire congregation bluntly, *"I do not believe what the Bible is saying about God and creation."* He was so proud of himself for defying the pastor. While the assembly was silent, an elderly lady stood up and asked the pastor softly if she could have a word with that young man. The pastor yielded to her with a sigh of relief. She took an apple from her purse and asked the young man to tell her whether or not the apple she had in her hand was sweet or sour. The young man replied with an annoying and arrogant tone, *"Madam, obviously you have a problem, how can I tell if your apple is sour or sweet since I have not tasted it?"* The old lady replied, *"This is exactly what your problem is. You cannot believe in God if you have not tasted Him or if you have not experienced Him."* And under the eyes of the young man, the elderly lady took a bite of her apple while the congregation applauded.

According to Blaise Pascal, it's the heart that feels God, not reason. According to Saint-Exupery, one sees clearly only with the heart … the essential is invisible to the eyes.

Believers always have said that those who do not believe but want to meet the Almighty or are looking for signs to accept his existence, need to open their hearts and the avenues of their thoughts. Just as one comes to believe in the existence of the wind without seeing it, the nuclear energy to the point of taking measures not to be exposed to it without physically seeing or touching it, there must be another dimension to understanding the concept of the divine. We do not need evidence to believe in God only because he cannot be apprehended by human reason. Woe is everyone who persists in trying to physically prove the existence of the everlasting God who transcends all areas of life. In the Christian race, the heart and brain in unison accept God. Jehovah surpasses all human logic.

Moreover, the explanations that we provide from science and history are not absolute truths. Yet, we examine the record and accept that which is most plausible. Eyewitnesses recount the same experience, and the same facts in different ways. The cathedral of knowledge by reason alone does not exist. According to Tennyson, "*… because nothing that is worth to be proven is provable or improvable, therefore, be wise and choose the sunniest side of the doubt.*" So why be so intransigent vis-à-vis the divine creed?

Rejection of God's Existence By Man

A. The Atheist

God transcends the human dimension. If he appeals to his copyright and files for a lawsuit, who would be the judge? Where can we find the jury pool? Suppose that God is the plaintiff, who is the defendant? The atheist?

If atheism is the doctrine that denies the absolute existence of God, then the trial cannot take place because one of the major parties is missing. If God shows up, the atheist would deny His presence, and if He does not show up, then He must be represented, but by whom? Usually, the lawyer of a given party is at least equally or better qualified than that of the other party. Who can amply represent God?

Someone whose existence is denied cannot represent Himself. Furthermore, according to Exodus 33:20, no man can see the LORD, and live.

B. What About The Agnostic?

If agnosticism recognizes the existence of a higher yet unnamed intelligence, then the debate cannot take place because the two parties cannot face each other.

Etymologically, the agnostic is defined as being ignorant, and not knowing enough about the superior intelligence.

C. The Nihilist

If nihilism is a doctrine that maintains that nothing exists in the absolute sense, it is the negation of all substantial reality and belief. Then again, we are forced to adjourn the trial 'indefinitely' or until the time of the ultimate Great Judgment that Jehovah has set himself to preside over. During that big day, the LORD declares that every man must answer for his choices, beliefs and attitude. Some say that good and evil are illusory, or that God has a dual power, or He is powerful but careless, etc. Wait for the end of their speech. Man is a finite being. In this new millennium of so many scientific advances, new techniques and ample discoveries, a great number of people use their freedom of choice and reason to reject God fully and openly, while ignoring or minimizing the Holy Scriptures. They espouse other theories and beliefs, some more imaginative and more sophisticated than others. Those who believe in God are accused of being simplistic, naive and even ignorant. One philosopher stated that he had to give up knowledge to embrace belief. Nowadays, countless numbers of people believe so, as if knowledge and faith were incompatible. Many are very proud to tell everyone that they never believed in, or no longer believe in a Supreme Being. They move among the disbelievers shamelessly. To address the question of the existence of God, first we must be discerning and of good faith.

D. Scientists and Their Support For The Big Bang

Scientists say: In the beginning ... Big Bang! What existed before the Big Bang? What caused it? Men still emit hypotheses, and theories. How can we be sure of the Big Bang? Have we seen it? How can we describe it? How can we flatly reject the God that gave us a credible manual to the benefit of a 'Big Bang' that we know so little about? How can intelligent people prefer to venture into the unknown to the detriment of data submitted by the Creator who provides the explanation for the world's existence? None of us was present. We must have faith in both cases. Scientists report many events to support their theory.

E. Scientists Say There Is No Place For God In The Universe

I dare to take a known example to illustrate man's dilemma: In 1988, a great British scientist — who received many awards and honours including the Presidential Medal of Freedom, the highest civilian honour in the United States in 2009 — the theoretical physicist and cosmologist Stephen William Hawking wrote a best-seller entitled *A Brief History of Time*. This book received various positive reviews. Among other things, the theoretical Physicist wrestled with the idea of wanting to find an explanation concerning why mankind and the universe exist. He went as far as to postulate that such a discovery would allow the scientists to 'know the mind of God'. With all due respect, this brilliant agnostic reasoning had a fundamental flaw; the premise itself is inappropriate. To explain the universe requires at least adequate knowledge about its content and components. So far, we have only just begun to learn about the universe. The more we know, the more there is to know. Then to postulate about it would be a projection of our own finite mind and nature on what we believe we see. The explanation we give may not necessarily be the correct interpretation of what we perceive. God never told us there was only one universe, one solar system. In fact, PSALMS 115:16 we read *"The heaven, even the heavens, are the Lord's: but the earth has he given to the children of men."* We make a lot of assumptions on our own, and as time goes by we learn from our trials and errors. In the future, we will learn even more and more. Those so-called 'redundant worlds' are strange to us in our current limited understanding of things. It's like a child saying, since we only have boy and girl, why do parents have 3, 5, or 10 children? We cannot apprehend God's way of thinking, reasoning, or behaving. We have our date of expiration. God has none. Now, about 12 years later, the renowned scientist is back with *The Grand Design* coauthored with the American scientist – Leonard Mlodinow. This time, Dr. Hawking believes *"It is not necessary to invoke God to light the blue touch paper and set the Universe going."* Is such a change of position due to frustration for not being able to 'know the mind of God'? This is a question that only God can answer. If the universe came out of nothing, we should not assume or use anything prior to its existence to explain it. If God does not exist for us, then we should not borrow anything that He may have brought into existence to explain our theories. Here again, the premise is false. How can you call upon natural laws, such as gravity to talk about spontaneous creation? Where do these laws come from? Which come first, the universe or the laws? One may argue, of course, the laws came first. Then how did these laws come about? Where does 'nothingness' come from? What steps were taken for 'nothingness' to be replaced by space occupying matter, and under what circumstances? Did 'nothingness' manage to transform itself into matter, energy? Why hasn't it been reproduced since then? Spontaneous creation, the process of evolution, cannot explain why the universe is the way it is and even seems to be expanding, or why there may be other universes? To put it simply, evolution and Big Bang cannot explain why our solar system and the earth are arranged in such exact way to allow mankind to live on this planet. Or is this just a lucky coincidence? All these theories require faith. God is so great, so mature that He gives man enough intelligence and reasoning to deny His existence. Nevertheless, man is a finite being, God is infinite. He does everything to maintain our privilege of being free to choose to have faith in Him or to believe in our theories. Isn't it strange that eminent scientists can theorize or even believe in the existence of extraterrestrial life, yet does not want to accept the existence of God? Can it be that we are so bright, so sophisticated that we cannot appreciate what is simple and obvious? At any rate, one should bear in mind that time is limitless, eternal for God. He has plenty of time to decide on what to do with the universe or the universes. It took scientists such as Jim Hartle and Hawking to postulate that the universe has 'no boundary in space-time', or Thomas Hertog and Hawking to propose a theory of 'Top Down Cosmology' meaning that the universe has no unique initial state. But simple believers have always known about black holes, limitless universe, and diversity in space because the Bible told us so. In fact, just read Job chapters 38, 39, 40 and 41. 1 Timothy 6:16 tells us that God only has immortality. He dwells in the light which no man can approach unto. No one has seen or can see God. According to Luke 1:37, there is nothing impossible to God. Jeremiah 32:17, tells us that nothing is too difficult for God.

F. The Consequences of Rejecting The Existence of God

Let us revisit the considerations made by our predecessors: Suppose that Jehovah does not exist. What is the implication? Everything has come into existence by chance through an evolutionary process that miraculously left the chaos of nothingness to achieve a masterpiece. Is this possible? Is it common sense? Have you seen things improve by themselves when you let them go at random? Try to abandon your garden, or your backyard for a season and see the result!

Consider the complexity of life: amino acids, proteins, DNA, micro motors inside cells, etc. Don't we believe that all life requires a source? The intellect, the complexity of the human organism, the nervous system and its ability to coordinate humans, or even the complexity of an eye, the gap in the fossil record … Is this the product of pure chance? An observation of the Milky Way, the enormity of the universe, all this should make man at least prudent, or even reconsider his theories on life and the existence of a Super Power. Some prefer their opinions and assumptions. According to 'science', all we see are the products of evolution that, over 15 billion years, have pushed the material to organize the Big Bang to the intelligence. We descend from galaxies, monkeys, bacteria — Those of us who are gifted with discernment and impartiality must admit that it takes faith to believe this theory. According to Kierkegaard, faith is a leap into the void. The theory of evolution speaks indirectly to herald a beginning by the 'Big Bang'.

G. Critics of God and His Existence

What are the reasons why some people deny the existence of God?

1. The idea of an invisible God whose will is revealed through the Bible is a puzzle that whetted people's curiosity. It is an intellectual challenge in a materialistic world. Man sees the Almighty through the prism of his humanity. Through anthropomorphism, he decided to capture what is elusive and wants to put it in his lab and analyze it.

2. The confusion caused by the emergence of religious pluralism combined with the misconduct or extreme attitudes of the so-called custodians and dispensers of various doctrines, make the same spiritual truth unstable and even a source of confusion. Any time people's behavior and action make others question their integrity, confidence is destroyed and the ring of fellowship is broken.

3. Self suggestion against the injustice, abuse, evil, sickness, death and cataclysm that are rampant in the world make man project onto God what he himself would have done if he were in God's position. Man cannot understand how a 'Being' as disciplined as God manages everything according to his established standards. He respects the autonomy and the free will of His creatures to the point of letting man choose freely even when the decisions of this creature are contrary to the wishes of the Creator and are detrimental to man's own welfare. Man's choices cause tremendous damage. Its impact leads to the ultimate sacrifice of that Creator to redeem his creation. *"O the depth of the riches both of the wisdom and knowledge of God!"* ROMANS 11:33a

4. It is politically correct to make fun of a Supreme Being who is not going to automatically react to the mockery of His creatures by demonstrating His omnipotence. Indeed, to mock God, to put his name in ridicule, and derision seems to make those who do it grow bigger and become more famous among the finest heads, scholars and world renowned people. It is fashionable and popular to slander God. Denying his existence puts you in big companies, among sophisticated people. This is the era of progress, when nearly everything can be explained scientifically, so why cling to the idea of a creator God that we cannot see? Therefore, believing in Him becomes a simple operation for the mentally challenged. It is childish to claim an association to such belief publicly. Some say it is a patent for ignorance; it is even medieval, according to others. But let us be sensible for a moment. If a child denies the existence of his parents once he can fend for himself, does this make him a hero? Even when he would lose his common sense and decide to do so, does this automatically force the parent to retaliate and do the same?

5. It is a clever attempt to escape the implications of the existence of God, because we believe if we confess, we must immediately implement our beliefs not only in ideology, but also to adopt a lifestyle that is consistent with our beliefs.

6. To doubt or deny the existence of God allows mankind to evolve peacefully in a permissive society of selfishness and self-sufficiency, where the pursuit of pleasure is paramount. Everywhere we turn, there is the encouragement to do as you want, to give free rein to your whims, to work to meet your needs without worrying about the consequences of the choices made. It is believed, or at least hoped that, after death everything is done forever. So we must enjoy life to the fullest.

7. Motivation, influence, the desire to be accepted and proselytizing also explain the rejection of God. People seem to be better valued by the intellectual elite when displaying his or her doubts. It places one in good company when you continue to seek for freedom, pleasure, wealth, and success by all means. We are even promoted, and rewarded, when we rebel against the values of orthodox religion.

8. To call yourself 'a believer' or a 'Christian', is unpopular in the secular world. The Christian is in his 'little shoes' or he feels minimized, ignored, mocked and even labeled as naive or ignorant. It has been really hard to take a stand for God.

9. Many are allergic to any spiritual notion because of a bad experience. Many people feel resentment because of a disaster, trauma, disease or death of a loved one. They expected God to intervene and act to save or heal. They are disappointed and angry at God who dared to disappoint them in such and such a circumstance. They argue that a good God could not tolerate so much evil, suffering, injustice and natural disasters.

These grievances are not caused by God, but because of the way things have become since sin came into this world. It is hard to believe, but the truth of the matter is, since we inherited sins from Adam and Eve, and God is infinitely pure and cannot deal with sin at all, the only thing that we deserve is destruction triggered by our sins. It is like an auto immune disease that triggers the auto-destruction of the organism. What we really deserve is God's wrath, but he is so merciful, that he sent his son to die on the cross to pay the penalty of sins, which is death. Then each time that our sins will activate our automatic destruction, Jesus' blood wipes out all those sins. This is the best 'antibiotic' against sins. The side effects are love, peace, joy, patience, but there is one simple 'catch', we must accept Christ. In other words, we must give our consent so to speak so Jesus can represent us and plead the case for us. Next time you meet someone who wants to curse and rebel against God because he or she 'has done nothing' to deserve all the bad things that are happening to her or him, please remind him or her that — by our human nature — we only deserve the worst. It is only through Jesus Christ that the worst turns into the best.

10. Some feel a certain disappointment in a God who is so slow and even inactive. Those who do not choose God believe he is inefficient, vague, distracted by other priorities: the wicked prosper, and those who are righteous languish in misery.

The role of mankind facing his ultimate destiny.

All in all, whatever we may say or think; whatever we desire, or hope for, we cannot dismiss what is beyond our grasp and our understanding.

In other words, our decision to believe or not to believe, can neither create, nor change or kill The Holy One. For, if he exists, our non-belief cannot eliminate him. If he does not exist, our belief cannot create him.

We cannot deny the existence of God based on emotions or disappointments. The Bible has never aspired to introduce a scientific presentation, or anatomical, physiological, or genetics ways to prove and explain God. It has only one objective, or approach, a narrative of everything the Creator made. Is the choice to accept Him for who He is, what He did or to reject Him, up to every one of us?

H. When Man Plays The Spoiled Child

We want a 100% guarantee, direct, quick interventions in order to be convinced that God exists. He is not Santa Claus that brings along what we wish for through the chimney. God cannot bend to our fantasies and our insatiable selfish desires upon command. This is not possible in this world. When I was a kid I remember hearing the story of a man who stood on a busy public place and challenged God. He said in a loud voice, *"God! If you really exist, I'm holding a dagger in one hand, use your power to slash my other hand!"* After motioning this, several times, he got no answer. Frustrated, the man put the knife to his neck and cried a little louder *"God! I give you one more chance, while everyone is watching and can hear me, if you really exist, order the knife to cut my throat and my neck to put an end to my poverty. I am ready to die, but the audience will believe in you after my death."* The man waited for a long time and nothing happened. Frustrated, he took off while hurling invectives against the Most High. One might ask, what sensible parent would have heard such a foolish request? If human beings who love their children would not do it, why expect that God would agree with him? The biggest dilemma of man is because he cannot understand the *modus operandi* of the Creator (how He operates).

According to ISAIAH 55:8, God's ways are not our ways, his thoughts are not ours. From 1 CORINTHIANS 1:25 we noted that even the 'foolishness' of God is wiser than the wisdom of the wisest person the world has ever known. According to the hint of an author, when we enter a plane from point **A** to reach point **B**, we have no guarantee that it will not crash before our arrival. However, when we take it, we are totally committed to whatever happens. We refuse to trust or stand for The Almighty. Suppose we do not have all the necessary evidence of the existence or nonexistence of God, but our commitment to accept or refuse such a concept determines our entire journey towards eternity. When we compare the challenge of the promises of eternal happiness or eternal destruction, frankly, it is worth placing your trust in the right Lord with a track record upon which he stands. Suppose that one of us meets a stranger (who happens to be Bill Gates perfectly disguised). He stopped one of us on the street and said in a friendly but determined voice: *"My friend, I promise you 1million dollars. Do you think I can give it to you?"* Anyone who is wise and intelligent is likely to say yes, after some hesitation. Why? Not only to show good manners and end the conversation, but if he says 'yes', the worst that can happen is he gets nothing. In fact, by saying yes he would lose nothing. If he says 'no' and the stranger (Bill Gates in disguise) can prove that he truly wanted to donate this large sum, this would be a great loss.

I. A Choice Much Easier Than One May Think

If we can take the risk of flying without the full guarantee of getting there, just to save time, or get involved in any activity, it is worth reflecting on the idea of a Creator who has set a genuine time for everything. He says that "… *to every purpose there is time and judgment…*" ECCLESIASTES 8:6. HEBREWS 9:27 says "… *it is appointed unto men once to die, but after this the judgment.*" How many people have predicted extraordinary things, and did not survive to see them happen in their lifetime? However, we have never seen God die. There is no grave and no mausoleum to see and honor his body. The biblical prophecies (spoken by God through his servants) were completed and fulfilled. Would it be worthwhile to think and choose? Who has seen a magnetic wave? Radiation and its effects exist and we believe or we will be its victims.

During the earthquake that hit the Republic of Haiti on January 12, 2010, thousands of people died and hundreds of thousands became traumatized, handicapped or homeless. Beneath the rubble were left numerous human bodies, countless precious objects, monuments and money. They were all destroyed in seconds. If we err, why not err on the side of caution and wisdom? What will happen to the eternal destiny of those who died suddenly in a natural disaster or another tragedy? All the victims have had the same fate, rich and poor, intellectuals and the illiterate, the upper class and the masses. The wealthy who lived in the most exclusive areas of the country in luxury and abundance would have given anything to spare their lives. Alas! When the death bell rings, people have to answer and no one can escape. The real question remains: does death announce the end of everything? This remains a wandering thought for all. None of the impressive bright scholars or great thinkers can provide a definitive answer to this important question. So why leave it up to chance? The

Bible itself says in REVELATIONS 1:18, Jesus, who is alive, holds the keys of death. In ECCLESIASTES 12:1 we read, *"Remember now thy Creator in the days of thy youth, while the evil days come not, nor the years draw nigh, when thou shalt say I have no pleasure in them."*

If we all know that we die, is death the last phase of human existence? This big question should provoke some serious thinking. The notion of God's existence is a matter of faith and a personal experience. It is a commitment that binds us to eternity. No one can be neutral. The difference between the believer and the unbeliever is simple — the believer relies on God and prefers to opt for eternal life, even risking the little favors that this current existence offers him. However, the non-believer takes his chance. He wants to build on his knowledge, intuition and cling to what he can see and touch in this world, even though it can disappear in a short time or upon his death. The believer has faith in his Creator, while the unbeliever has faith in human's theories. Has man ever erred in his knowledge of things? Of course. Do people who die ever come back to life? Of course not. Can you lose everything, including your own life in the blink of an eye? Yes, but the Almighty never errs. It would be wise to lean in the direction of the believers. The Bible says in NUMBERS 23:19 that *"God is not a man that he should lie; neither the son of man, that he should repent."* Everything he says, he will do. What he has done so far is no secret. ROMANS 4:21 invites us to be fully convinced that whatever he promises he can fulfill. If we err, why not wander in the direction of reason or 'the probability of God'? This could be the first step toward further choice and action towards a new and meaningful life.

J. The Existential Challenge of Pascal

Consider for a moment the existential challenge of Pascal:

Scenario Number One: God exists. When the end of all things happens, He will judge the world. If you have shared such a belief, your conviction and faithfulness will be upheld and rewarded. You will participate in the eternal kingdom whence will flow milk and honey, happiness and everlasting life. *"Where God himself will wipe away every tear from the eyes of his elect. Death will be no more, and there will be no more mourning or crying or pain"*, according to REVELATION 7:17, 21:4.

Scenario Number Two: God exists. You do not believe in Him. What a terrible surprise for you to meet and face the trial and the eternal verdict. What argument will you have to clear yourself? How can He be more gracious to you at this fateful moment when you spent your entire life ignoring Him? It would be unfair, given the fact that His followers spoke to you about judgment Day. You never listened. At the end He will give you what you deserve. The fate that is reserved for nonbelievers is clearly described in the Bible; it is eternal destruction. REVELATIONS 21:8 says, "*But the fearful, and unbelieving, and the abominable, and murderers, whore mongers, and sorcerers, and idolaters and all liars, shall have their part in the lake which burns with fire and brimstone, which is the second death.*" According to this text and HEBREWS 9:27, after having lived on this earth, it is for everyone to die, then at the end of time the trial leading to the second death, total annihilation, or everlasting rewards begins. Do not say that the Lord is vengeful. He made ample provision for the redemption of mankind to the point of giving His own life on the cross for our salvation. My friends, what more could He have done?

Scenario Number Three: God does not exist, but you believed in Him. At the end of all things, there is nothing. You're dead. You do not wake up. Nothing is happening. You are in the unconscious state. The dust cannot feel regret. You really have not lost or gained anything. You do not exist to enjoy your choice.

Scenario Number Four: God does not exist. You did not believe in Him. Your disbelief is 'justified' but you will not be aware. Death has been the end of all existence and all things. You will not have the privilege to feel vindicated because you will not be conscious. Therefore, everything depends on whether or not we believe that God exists. If, for argument's sake, He does not exist, at the end of life, nobody has won or lost because all of us turn into dust. We will have disappeared forever. Every man dies and it is the end, even those who believed in the existence of God. They are finished once they return to nothingness. However, if God exists, as the Bible, nature, and our conscience dictate, if there is a Last Judgment and a verdict or a reward according to our rejection or acceptance of salvation, then the rebels will thread trouble and fear. *"Men's hearts failing them for fear, and for looking after those things which are coming on the earth: for the powers of heaven shall be shaken. And then shall they see the Son of man coming in a cloud with power and great glory,"* LUKE 21:26,27. Why persist in one direction? It's up to you.

K. The Choice Is Really Simple

Man, as a sensible being, chooses to err on the side of the highest probability. Can we risk an ever lasting life because of the probability that after death there is nothingness? And if as the Bible says, after death comes the day of reckoning, where will you be? Where will I be? What will be our fate? Bear in mind that the authentic doctrine is not the key to God's kingdom. He does not require any meritorious work. Just believe and accept the offer of salvation. Everything is already paid for. The believers accept the fact that God exists and that he rewards those who seek him, according to HEBREWS 11:6. The Bible reflects the ardent desire of heaven to save us if we accept the salvation that is offered to us. Allow the following illustration, although simplistic: suppose a normal human being endowed with his entire physical and mental faculty experiences hunger. You can get food for him, and even bring it to his mouth, but he must open his mouth, chew and swallow what he is given. He has to make a contribution or provide a minimum of collaboration. According to the Bible, God did everything for our salvation. We need only to accept it and believe in him. *"Not of works, lest any man should boast."* EPHESIANS 2:9. For a clearer idea of the free offer of salvation, you can consult other texts, including: PSALMS 31:16, *"Make thy face to shine upon thy servant: save me for thy mercies' sake."* ROMANS 11:6, *"And if by grace, then is it no more of works: otherwise grace is no more grace. But if it be of works, then it is no more grace: otherwise work is no more work."* II CORINTHIANS 9:8 and 15, *"And God is able to make all grace abound toward you; that ye, always having all sufficiency in all things, may abound to every good work … Thanks be unto God for his unspeakable gift."*

You can also read the following texts: PROVERBS 22:1, ROMANS 5:17, EXODUS 33:19, ISAIAH 30:18, EPHESIANS 4:7, 2 TIMOTHY 1:9, HEBREWS 4:16, 1 CORINTHIANS 15: 10, 1 PETER 5:5, EPHESIANS 5:20, and TITUS 3:7. In JOHN 5:24, Jesus said when he was on earth, *"Verily, verily, I say unto you, whoever hears my word and believes in him who sent me, has everlasting life, and shall not come into condemnation ; but is passed from death unto life."* ***"Behold, I stand at the door, and knock: If any man hear my voice and open the door, I will come in to him, I will sup with him, and he with me."*** REVELATION 3:20.

 Plea For Faith

a.) Have we ever seen a Cadillac leaving the factory spontaneously coming out of no where and made up of nothing? How can we accept the theory that this well organized universe, our world came out of nowhere and organized itself? An atom is complicated, fascinating and full of intelligence. None of us was present in the beginning, neither the believers in God, nor those who believe in the Big Bang. We cannot comprehend the Creator or explain his ways and means or fully know his thinking pattern and actions. If we could do so, he would cease to be God. Moreover, we can choose to believe in a Creator for his divinity and magnificent prowess and operations during creation or believe in the theory of evolution and its proposals and speculations. In either case, we cannot answer all questions. However, we can demonstrate common sense and ask: which is more plausible? If by faith we needed to choose between the two, which one is more plausible? Which one offers less risk to our ultimate destiny? In PSALMS 14:1 it is said, *"The fool says in his heart, there is no God."* JEREMIAH 10:6-12 *"Forasmuch as there is none like unto thee O LORD; thou art great, and thy name is great in might. Who would not fear thee, O King of nations?"* The constancy of the laws that govern the creation, its beauty and its size, should arouse our admiration. His arrangement, dimensions as infinitely small as they are infinitely large, and the complexity and richness of nature suggest at least a dependence on a supreme being.

b.) The way evil predominates across the land suggests a need for an opposing force that is good, as negative is opposed to positive, darkness is opposed to light, and evil is contrary to good. If only evil exists, then why do we complain when things go wrong? Any good thing or deed would be the effect of chance and a malformation of the strain of evil. The normal man expects and longs for good deeds. He feels a deep physiological and emotional satisfaction in doing good. The very fact of wanting to blame Jehovah for what is evil shows a certain tacit acceptance of the desire for good deeds. Who are we to determine the basis for the administration of the Sovereign Master and his functions in the universe? God had to ask Job in Job 38:4, "*Where were you when I founded the earth ?*" Job 11:7 says, "*… canst thou by searching find out God?*"

A. God's Faithfulness and Constancy Confirm His Existence.

All of us know that tomorrow the sun will break forth in the distance. We cannot guarantee the level of its influence, but everyone knows that all over the land, the sun will rise from the east to tell us hello. Even if you and I no longer live to see it, we know it will rise. We do not need to prove it. Similarly we do not need absolute certainty to believe in God. Just like the sun or wind, or snow, or magnetic fields, or nuclear radiation, the existence of God does not depend on human ability to manipulate or control him.

If a son decides that his father does not exist, the father does not have the obligation to reveal himself to the son. Because of values and ethics, the father may take steps to ensure his son's survival and well being until he is able to make decisions and pay for the consequences of his choices. It is the same for God.

Matthew 5:45 says, *"He makes his sun to rise on the evil and on the good, and sends rain on the just and on the unjust."* He wants to be among those who believe in Him and give Him the praise and respect He deserves. He is not needed by those who choose greed instead of peace and harmony. He cannot be the 'fly in the soup', or the unwelcome guest. You know, there is general revelation to all; nature is an open book that can be read and understood by all, regardless of their intelligence, language, race, age, gender or class. The Supreme Master makes the sun rise across the world. He gives rain in its time, etc. He is willing to prove to everyone individually, as a father who wants not only to provide the basic needs for his sons or daughters, but also wants a special relationship with his descendants. Even if a parent has a lot of kids, he maintains a unique relationship with each of them. The child must believe in his parent. With God, it cannot be otherwise. He gives us what is necessary to cope with this life. The rest is up to us. Everything depends on us and this is individual and unique for everyone. When someone obtains his license to drive, you do not give him a Ferrari to get started. Our relationship with God is personal and progressive. The results arise from our continuous relationship and contacts with the Creator. He is available for everyone. It is up to us to decide on what we want to do with God in our lives.

We admit that some facts in the Bible are difficult to explain and perplex us, some interventions or non-intervention from the supernatural make us wonder. The responses do not always correspond to our expectations. They are not yet within our reach because of our level of spiritual growth. **Let us remember that our spiritual**

growth is not measured by the yardstick of our IQ or our socioeconomic status. God takes pleasure in honoring the contrite and humble hearts. These are the exceptions that prove the rule. We must accept that GOD is sovereign. He is omnipotent and omniscient. He has always been in control of things. REVELATIONS 1:8 says, *"I am Alpha and Omega, the beginning and the ending, saith the Lord, which is, and which was, and which is to come, the Almighty."* You can also see 1 TIMOTHY 6:15, PSALMS 83:19, and EPHESIANS 1:28 ...

B. **If You Believe, Approach Him Without Fear**

In the religious domain, two approaches are in order:

1. **The rational theology** through which people reach a level where they can at least accept certain beliefs that come straight from observation and innate intuition. Viewpoints are accepted wholeheartedly because they make sense for them.

2. **The revealed theology** drawn from astute study of the Holy Scriptures with prayers and humility. Natural man often begins with the rational theology, but he must move forward and get to the theology revealed that has as a unique source the teaching of biblical doctrines. Salvation is simple — We recognize our condition as sinners, accept Jesus by faith to give us salvation (justification by faith), and let Christ continue the appropriate transformation in us (sanctification). Even if our actions pivot around rationalization, they should lead to a closer relationship between us and God. He reveals Himself to all His creation through the scope, brilliance and magnificence of His works. Yet He does not force anyone to accept Him. You must realize that the time will come when everyone will be accountable before the throne of the almighty.

C. When God's Action May Seem 'Strange' To Us

Like you, I have had moments of doubt and questioning, so I speak to Him directly. I still believe He is sovereign. Instead of speaking of God, I talk to God. Instead of complaining about Him, I present my complaints to Him directly and I am comforted by the mere fact of having established communication with Him. **For even the silence of God is a form of response to my queries.** Job had the same experience. JOB 42:5, 6 says, *"My ears had heard of You but now my eye sees You. That is why I condemn and I repent in dust and ashes."* After the 1,001 complaints, God finally revealed Himself to Job, not to explain, but to question him. Job 40:1, 2 says, *"And the Lord answered Job out of the whirlwind and said: gird your loins like a man I will demand of thee, and thou Me."* If we read the book of Job in the Bible, we notice that in Job's restoration, the Lord gave him much more than he had before. God never explained to Job why he had to go through so much. He did not say why Job had to endure so much hardship. The vicissitudes of life are measured for everyone of us according to who we are and what we can or cannot handle.

After an overwhelming day, I was tired and eager to go home for a little rest. Just as I threw myself on the bed, the phone rang. The person at the other end informed me that one of my cousins had a car accident. He received a blow to the head and was in the emergency room. I was very upset and anxious. I already had a long list of unanswered questions for God, and that one threw me overboard. I even dared to question His control of the Earth. I became literally furious, delirious. A thousand thoughts were competing for supremacy in my brain. None of them was honorable. Shortly after, I learned that an MRI of the brain had revealed that my cousin had a brain tumor that was developing. In other words, had it not been for the car accident, he would not have had the MRI. Without that accident, that tumor could have taken much longer to be detected. It could have been too late, or may be after a fatal accident because my cousin uses the highway daily and at least five times a week. Can you imagine what could have happened? Sometimes we cannot accept defeat or bad news, but what matters most is our attitude toward God in the midst of the furnace of trials and tribulations. Can we pass or fail the tests?

I remember when my son, at 3 years old, urged me to get him a 'grown up' bicycle with all the fancy gadgets and accessories for him to ride on the streets like 'all the big people', he kept repeating. He made this request many times and with insistence. Each time, I told him 'no', but he could not even understand my explanation because he was too young to grasp reality.

Our prospects of things are limited. There is often a wall that prevents us from seeing the other side. Our vision is too opaque to see what is looming on the horizon. We can only know or understand partly. Let's trust Him! Like Job, the time will come when we have the answer to all our questions. St. Paul, one of the greatest intellectuals of his time, was a fervent believer. He said in 1 CORINTHIANS 13:9 that today we know in part until what is perfect is introduced.

D. Faith: A Close and Personal Path With God

Allow me to submit to you another example of my limited spiritual perspective. Family life is a journey full of surprises. Everyone can remember a number of challenges that have marked his or her life. I still remember my wife's second pregnancy. Like the first, it was very difficult. She was among those called 'high-risk pregnancies' with gestational diabetes, and various symptoms of 'pre-eclampsia'. Therefore, she had to be followed by one of the best doctors in obstetrics and gynecology, and an endocrinologist. Her obstetrician was in Manhattan. His office was equipped with everything a medical office could dream of having, except maybe a bit of heart and understanding.

Because of her health, it was clear that my wife could not continue to work. Therefore, from the beginning, we had to take the necessary steps to let the medical insurance company know and file for possible disability. Unfortunately, because of the tasks added to being new parents (our first baby was premature and the children were only a few months apart; I was going to medical school, etc.), we failed to file the form on time. Our application was finally and officially rejected for having submitted the documents too late. This was a big financial blow to us. How and where would we find the money to survive, let alone pay one of the best specialists for medical care? We continued to go for the second and third visits with a lot of apprehension because we knew we had no money to pay the doctor. At the end of the fourth monthly visit, the receptionist / nurse called me in front of all the other patients, as if she were using a microphone or she thought I was deaf, to tell me through her glasses hanging on her nose, *"Mr. François, it is time to start paying the doctor if you expect him to deliver your baby. If by next visit you cannot come up with at least two thirds of the money, the doctor will not be able to continue to see your wife*". I was stunned! You cannot imagine our embarrassment in the presence of all those pregnant women and their husbands. All eyes were looking at me and my poor wife. I wanted to dig a hole and bury us instantly. I do not know how we found the strength to get out of the office that day. As I was drying the tear drops that were running down my wife's face, we undertook the long way home, without exchanging a word. It was not necessary. We knew it was our time to make our '911 call of faith'. Our moral existence was on fire and we desperately needed a miracle. Once we arrived home, we prayed and I left the house without knowing where I was going. I had to take a walk quickly. There are times you cannot stay home like an invalid. It was as if I wanted to salvage the bare minimum of my dignity. When I returned, I got the mail and presented it to my wife who was already in bed. She cast a quick glance at the mail and threw them on her dressing table with disdain, and laid down again. Nearly a week passed and we kept thinking but we could not come up with a solution. We had no idea where we were going to get the money to go back to that office and regain our pride. We continued to discuss, seek and pray, but we remained clueless. Not a single sign of deliverance. The following weekend, my mother-in-law came in and decided to clean the house. She asked my wife about the envelopes left on the dresser. My wife told her to get rid of them. My mother-in-law had curiosity mixed with wisdom and opened them before throwing them out. Guess what was in one of them? In one of the envelopes from the insurance company, that had previously rejected wife's application for disability, was a check. It got even better. Guess how much the check was for? Exactly the amount we needed to pay the doctor.

Somehow the insurance company had declined the application earlier in order to accumulate the amount for my wife's disability until it reached the amount we needed, at the exact time it was needed to save us from our embarrassment. We almost threw that envelope in the garbage. If we were receiving the money biweekly or monthly, we would have spent it as it came, and we would not have the money for the obstetrician. The following week we were very proud to return to the office and tell the nurse as loud as we could, *"Here is the check with the full amount for the doctor!"*

Was this a coincidence or divine intervention? I have my beliefs. What is yours? According to PROVERBS 16:7, when the Lord approves your way, when he has mercy on you, he can use even your enemies to come to your rescue.

Through Jesus, serving the Creator includes disappointment, pain, abuse, humiliation, and even death. God is still omnipotent, he loves us. ROMANS 8:35 indicates that nothing should separate us from the love of God. Often the difficulties for which we blame God are not caused by Him, but He allows them to happen for our spiritual growth and development. Alas! How often do we respond with murmurs, frustrations, or accusations or blasphemy? We must learn to manage our emotions.

E. A Personal Appeal

Yes dear beloved, take an inventory of your life. Look back. How many times have you overcome serious challenges? Do you think you went through it alone? As you read these pages, maybe you are suffering from a disease, you are going through a difficult time, you have burning issues and you cannot find any answer that is humanly possible. I challenge you to try the Almighty! JEREMIAH 29:11 says *"I know the thoughts that I think towards you, said the Lord, thoughts of peace, and not of evil, to give you an expected end."*

My friend, maybe you do not believe in God. Perhaps the trials and tribulations have weakened your faith or your way of life separates you from Him. For whatever reason, I invite you to be honest with yourself. Do not rest your eternal life on a simple probability. It is time for you to bring yourself to Him. I assure you He will do a miracle and He will reveal himself to you one way or another, if you are sincere. Have faith in God. You can even read this model of dialogue with the Supreme Being:

"O God, in my words, my thoughts or my actions, my life is mushrooming with questions and challenges. Please come in this moment and reveal yourself to me personally in whatever way possible. Since you love me, show me that love. Amen."

Synoptic View on The Concept of Religion

Definition of religion

Etymologically, the word religion, *religio* in Latin, means 'careful attention, reverence', or *relegere, religere*, to gather, collect, present a reverent worship. Religion is the set of beliefs, values, opinions and attitudes of man vis-à-vis supernatural beings to which much reverence is given. Every religion reflects a belief in a being or a higher principle, the role of the creature, and the creed. In the creed we can include the laws and precepts of religion as well as the rites and customs of belonging

Religions and their origins.

The causes and genesis of religion are not universally accepted. Primitive religion sprouted from challenges, circumstances and human illusions. Primitive men seemed to adore everything they could identify. They translated their concerns into worshipping rocks, hills, mountains, plants, trees, animals, the various elements of nature, celestial bodies, etc. Through history, the impulse to worship was evident everywhere but in different ways. The debate about the origin of monotheistic or polytheistic religion continues. We leave it to contemporary students and scholars to continue the discussion initiated by a long list of bright people, including Plato, Aristotle, Socrates, Protagoras, Galileo, St. Thomas Aquinas, Descartes, Kant, Auguste Comte, Pascal, Durkheim, Nietzsche, Marx, Weber, and many more. The key is that every society — regardless of its geographical position, its sphere of influence and its culture – adopts some form of religion, even when denying it. Individually, everyone has his values, beliefs or religion. Among the most widespread religions on earth, let us note briefly:

Overview of various religions.

1. Pagan religions that some people believe came into existence because of the innate tendency in man to worship. Here, 'Pagan religions' means a range of spiritual practices, religious traditions based on deities, objects, superstitions, nature, and magical attributes to various things with one thing in common, a plurality of sources of worship, many gods and/or objects.

2. Polytheistic religions, or religions that promote several gods, such as:

> *a.* Hinduism: 'self cosmic' where the human being is part of what is complete, yet impersonal. There are a multitude of deities.
>
> *b.* Buddhism which believes that the universe has evolved. The gods are temporal, and the ultimate goal is to eradicate hatred, mistakes/error and desire.
>
> *c.* Some other religions, including New Age.

3. Monotheistic religions that believe in one God, the Creator of the universe. They are:

> *a.* Judaism: Yahweh is the unique God who revealed himself to his servants, the patriarchs and prophets to communicate his will to his chosen

people, the Jews, who continue to await the coming of The Messiah.

b. Islam, where Allah used a man, Muhammad, to reveal his will.

c. Christianity, God became man in the person of his son, Jesus Christ, to reveal his love for the human race. He died in our place to expiate our sins.

Even within Christianity, we have the Orthodox, Anglicans, and Protestants who in turn have several subdivisions, most of whom do not like being classified as Protestant sects.

4. In some places, religion is directly related to the culture of the population, such as, China, Persia, Japan, and India.

Christianism.

Since we live in a culture generally considered as Christian, this book is intended for believers of Christianity whose authentic author is Jesus Christ. To do justice to history, Jesus Christ, during his sojourn on this earth, never formed a specific religion. The message he wanted to spread was rather simple: mankind, which was created to have a life of joy and peace, disobeyed, and therefore became separated from God the Creator who is immaculate. The eternal Son came into this world to redeem mankind and reconcile him with the Holy Father. Jesus offered himself as ransom for the salvation of the world. He declares in LUKE 19:10, that *"The Son of Man is come to seek and to save that which was lost."*

Overview of Christianity.

To respect the historical context of Christianity, we must admit it came out of Judaism because Jesus Christ himself was born and lived as a Jew. His place of birth, mother, name, career, and ultimate fate, followed by his triumph after his crucifixion, was predicted. MICAH 5:2 *"But thou, Bethlehem Ephratah, though thou be little among the thousands of Judah, yet out of thee shall he come forth unto me that is to be ruler in Israel; whose goings forth have been from of old, from everlasting."*

ISAIAH 9:65 *"For unto us a child is born, unto us a son is given: and the government shall be upon his shoulder: and his name shall be called Wonderful, Counselor, The mighty God, The everlasting Father, The Prince of Peace."* ISAIAH 35:4 *"Say to them that are of a fearful heart, Be strong, fear not: behold, your God will come with vengeance, even God with a recompense; he will come and save you."*

ISAIAH 53:12 *"Therefore will I divide him a portion with the great, and he shall divide the spoil with the strong; because he hath poured out his soul unto death: and he was numbered with the transgressors; and he bare the sin of many, and made intercession for the transgressors."* PSALMS 22:16 *"For dogs have compassed me: the assembly of the wicked have inclosed me: they pierced my hands and my feet."* PSALM 16:10 *"For thou wilt not leave my soul in hell; neither wilt thou suffer thine Holy One to see corruption."*

The creed of Christianity.

Christianity believes in one God who manifests Himself gradually with the location, time and circumstances, but the principles remain forever. He created everything for His glory. He has done everything to make man happy. He created man with the freedom to choose what is best and also with the potential to choose the worst. When, in the Garden of Eden, man opted for the worst and disobeyed, in His great love, the Creator decided to redeem man by sending His only son to suffer the consequences of his disobedience, and grant absolution access to eternal life. EPHESIANS 2:8, 9 says, *"By grace ye are saved, through faith; and that not of yourselves: it is the gift from God: not of works, lest any man should boast." "No flesh shall be justified by the deeds of the law."* (ROMANS 3:20). Before Jesus came to this earth to save us, Noah, and Abraham found grace in the eyes of the Lord (ROMANS 4:3, 13). The idea of man saving himself by his deeds has never been biblical. It is inherited from pagans' religions and likely found its way into Christianity, most significantly after the massive conversion from paganism to Christianism under the leadership of Constantine during the 5th century.

However, after having been absolved, the Christian must change his way of living. He is saved by grace and through faith. He must resolve to profess that faith by walking in the new-found path provided to him by the one who died for him. He may slumber or fall here and there, but his new engagement is a daily experience. It is progressively solidified via his walk with God, who renews his commitment and fortifies his will to the point when sin becomes something he can no longer take pleasure in committing. The blessed Redeemer plans to give the regenerated man, saved by grace, access to the restored Eden. Then, the original plan that was put on hold by sin, will be implemented fully and man will live in perfect harmony with his creator, where there will be no more suffering, disease or mortality. The most important challenge for authentic Christianity is to cultivate good relations with God and with his neighbor.

Christianity through the ages.

The person who wants to keep track of the history and theology of Christianity should have no difficulty accepting God as the author. Only God deserves to be worshipped. For more than 2,000 years, after the founding of Christianity, the same practice continues. The Church had moments of trouble through the ages, certainly, but its dissemination and preservation remain firm. It has survived all those who predicted its destruction. The blood of martyrs has been used as a seed for its prosperity and stainability. How did Christianity manage to spread and stay alive? Jesus used the very nature of man, a sociable being who operates within a community. When a group of individuals decide to help each other by sharing the same goals, ideals, and beliefs, nothing can hinder its success. It is also the same and even better spiritually. This is how the main concept of 'Christian assembly' was developed. It is paramount to remain among whole hearted followers. Even then, the main source, the ultimate model to follow, is Jesus Christ. Authentic Christianity, or any religion, becomes tainted and divided when irregenerate people with ulterior motives infiltrate and cause disarray or a deviation from the right and narrow path. This is why I personally challenge every believer to beware of cults, churches, and faith-based organizations that require people to submit themselves blindly under the pretense of learning or allegiances. Only God deserves our unconditional obedience and our undisputed allegiance. Only the truth provides authority and requires obedience and respect.

The Church In The Old Testament Era

In order to really grasp the connection between God, man and the church, it is worth going back to the beginning of creation in the first chapters of Genesis.

Genesis 1:27 tells us that God created man in His image and after his likeness. In verse 31 we read, *"And God saw everything that he had made, and, behold, it was very good."*

a.) **Genesis 3:8** states that, *"And they heard the voice of the LORD God walking in the garden in the cool of the day: and Adam and his wife hid themselves from the presence of the LORD God amongst the trees of the garden."* Why? The answer most likely supposes an attachment felt by the Creator toward his creatures. He wants to speak with the couple. Imagine the King of Kings, whom the heaven of heavens cannot contain, who took pleasure in being reduced to a level compatible with the reception of Adam and Eve as special guests. We even dare to infer that it was like a regular vesper's rendezvous when God and his two children met and were talking. Then one evening, as usual, the Lord went into the garden, at the same place at the same time for the heart-to-heart conversation. This time, the couple was not ready to receive Him. Adam and Eve hid themselves. The text of Genesis 3:9 continues, *"And the LORD God called unto Adam, and said unto him, where art thou?"*

Do you think Adam and Eve could hide from Him "*...for whom everything is naked and exposed?*" (HEBREW 4:13). The question that God asked Adam, "*Where are you?*" will be repeated in a different way. To Moses, it was, "*What have you in your hands?*", To Elijah it was, "*What are you doing here?*" This same voice later will cry in MATTHEW 11:28, as "*Come unto Me, all ye that labour and are heavy laden, and I will give you rest.*" Or, "*O Jerusalem, Jerusalem, thou that killest the prophets, how often would I have gathered thy children together, even as a hen gathereth her chickens under her wings, and ye would not!*" (MATTHEW 23:37). This expresses the love and desire to convince man that the Creator is always seeking for a cordial dialogue with him, such a conversation must be sought and wanted by man. In light of these verses, we can conclude that God created man to talk with him. He wants to instruct, and direct man's life toward eternal bliss, but he would never take away man's right to choose freely.

In GENESIS 4:9, God said to Cain, "*Where is your brother Abel?*" Once again we see a father who cares about the welfare and actions of his children. He advises them to avoid evil and choose good without violating their freedom.

b.) **In GENESIS 6:5,** "*The Lord saw that the wickedness of man was great in the Earth, and all thoughts of their hearts were only evil continually.*"

We know that God and evil cannot coexist. When man chose evil, he rejected God who was forced to let him experience the cost of his choice. He approached Enoch, and began to take care of him, but his generation was not interested in spiritual things. In

Genesis 6:6, it is said, *"The Lord repented that he had made man on earth, and He was grieved in his heart."* These words are used to place God in the human dimension to allow us to grasp his love. God experienced the same affliction, the sadness felt by every parent when he or she sees his or her child give up the advantages of home and family to follow the advice of friends who do not have their best interest at heart. To insist on further and deeper involvement with evil, could only irritate the Creator. Man knew about the experience of the flood. Genesis 8:20 tells us that after the flood, Noah built an altar to the Lord and this gave Him great pleasure. God said he would no longer destroy mankind with a flood.

c.) **Genesis 12** reveals a God who did not abandon the plan to share friendship, and companionship with man. This time, he spoke to Abram. Reading Genesis 12:7, 8, and Genesis 13:4, we see that Abram (whose name was changed to Abraham by God in Genesis 17:5) did not follow the customs or culture of his country. Instead, he listened to the voice of the Creator. On his path, every time the Lord came into contact with Abram, — whether in Shechem or Bethel, Abram built an altar and called upon the name of the Lord. According to Genesis 13:18, Abram built an altar to Jehovah among the oaks of Mamre, near Hebron. Genesis 14:20 indicates Abram met Melchizedek, King of Salem, priest of God Most High and Abram tithed. In Genesis 15, Jehovah promised to give Abram and his descendants the possession of Canaan. Genesis 15:13, God told Abram that because of human wickedness, his descendants would be enslaved for 400 years.

d.) **The biblical story** reveals that at that appointed time, God raised up Moses who abruptly ordered Pharaoh to let the people go. Pharaoh resisted, but after the 10 plagues, including the death of his eldest son, Pharaoh reluctantly had to let the descendants of Abraham go as God had promised. But on their way to the promise land, what a saga! A sequence of events had marked that journey. After crossing the Red Sea miraculously with dry feet, Exodus 15 tells us that Moses and the Israelites sang a song unto the Lord. In Exodus 20, the Lord enacted his law to teach the people how to serve him. In EXODUS 25:8 The Lord declared, *"They make me a sanctuary, and I will dwell among them."* In the first verse of the same chapter (EXODUS 25), it is permissible to discover that it was Yahweh himself who gave the orders to build the sanctuary. He took care to provide all the details for building the tabernacle and its operation, the ark, the candlestick, those who were to officiate, when and how, etc.

In EXODUS 25, 26, 31, He again gave details for the construction of the Tabernacle, the choice of priests, offerings, and sacrifices in his honor. Everything was dictated by Jehovah.

EXODUS 40:38 says, *"The cloud of the LORD was upon the tabernacle by day, and night, there was a fire in the eyes of the whole house of Israel throughout all their journeys."*

We should ask the following question, Why had God gone through so much trouble to be in the company of humans in spite of their disobedience and, shortcomings? The simple answer is, *"I have loved thee with an everlasting love; therefore with loving kindness have I drawn thee."* (JEREMIAH 31:3). He loved them.

He wanted to fulfill the promise made to Abram, who became Abraham, who remained faithful to the limits of his possibilities. Better yet, God kept his fundamental principle, that man was created for His glory. No being can exist apart from the creator. In return, God requires one thing: to be **worshipped and obeyed**.

He deserves it by right of creation and redemption and because of the promise of eternal salvation. Man can use his freedom and create his own god, when he chooses to exist outside of a relationship with his Creator deliberately. Moreover, when the creature prefers his own life, partner, offspring, his parents, family members, friends, property, employment, money, vacations, and pleasures above God his maker, this shows his ungratefulness and lack of respect along with poor judgment. Yet, the Creator continues to show him His love because His sole purpose is to provide happiness to His creatures. Since the creation, God has decided to share humans' company not because of their personal merits, but because of His unwavering love for them. He wanted to be with them through the tabernacle. A God that the whole universe cannot contain, who should be very busy managing the whole universe — humanly speaking, here He is, reserving a special time for this group of former slaves, the Israelites.

In Leviticus 23, the High One took the trouble to describe the offerings and sacrifices, festivals and invitations — everything that pertains to His relationship with people. As for the book of Numbers, we found countless examples. They include: The function and enumeration of the Levites Numbers 4:48.

In NUMBERS 7: the offerings of the tribal leaders for the dedication of the tabernacle.

In NUMBERS 8: the consecration of the Levites.

In NUMBERS 35: the Levitical cities, etc.

The book of Deuteronomy contains similar recommendations.

In DEUTERONOMY 8:17,18 are the warnings and cautions not to forget the Lord, and believe themselves to be the author of their success.

In DEUTERONOMY 14 and 16, instructions after instructions were provided, telling the people not to engage in harmful practices that would force the Lord to abandon them.

In DEUTERONOMY 32, we read the Song of Moses.

In DEUTERONOMY 33, Moses blessed the children of Israel before his death.

In DEUTERONOMY 34, Moses died on Mount Nebo in Moab, 120 years old in full health. The Lord buried him in the valley in the land of Moab. But the Lord did not abandon His people.

e.) **Before Moses' death**, it was revealed to Moses who Yahweh had chosen to succeed him. He proceeded to hand over the power to **Joshua**. Joshua took over and led the people to the conquest of Canaan, the passage of Jordan, and the subjugation of Jericho. In JOSHUA 8:30, after the capture of Jericho, Joshua built an altar to the Lord on Mount Ebal. If we take our time to scrutinize the Bible, we note that according to biblical accounts, more than 400 altars were built in the Old Testament to honor the Lord.

f.) **After Joshua**, throughout the existence of Israel with the judges, priests and prophets, Jehovah Nissi was always present among His children, despite their imperfections.

g.) **In 1 SAMUEL 8**, the Israelites demanded a king from Samuel. They wanted to imitate the example of other nations around them. They were tired of the theocratic regime. In 1 SAMUEL 8:7, 8, *"The Lord said to Samuel: Look, the people's voice in everything you say, because it's not you they reject, it's Me that they reject, so I should not reign over them. They act towards you as they have always done since I've made up out of Egypt until this day, they have* ***forsaken Me****, to serve other gods."*

The Lord allowed Samuel to choose Saul as the first king of Israel, then his successor, David. Once he became king, David took the ark, according to 2 SAMUEL 6:1, 2.

"David again gathered all the elite of Israel, numbering 30,000 men. And David, with all the people that were with him, marched to the ark of God, which is invoked before the name of the LORD of hosts which resides between the cherubim above the ark." David wanted to build a temple for the Lord (2 SAMUEL 7:1-12).

What did the King of Kings say to David? Yes, but not you, David. Send, your son instead, Solomon (2 SAMUEL 7:13). David passed the guidelines and provided materials for the construction of the temple by his son Solomon.

1 Kings 6, described the construction of the temple. In 1 Kings 9:3 is the story of the dedication. *"And the Lord said unto him, I have heard thy prayer and thy supplication, that thou hast made before me: I have hallowed this house, which thou hast built, to put my name there for ever; and mine eyes and mine heart shall be there perpetually."* To better understand the divine intervention, please read the prayer of Solomon in 1 Kings 8. Nevertheless, throughout their history, people continued to rebel against God. They had to pay the consequences for such scourges: captivity, disease, disasters, death, and destruction of the temple. Yet, the Father Almighty never gave up on sharing the company of humans. He remained sensitive to the prayers of those who were faithful both individually and in groups. I cite as evidence the prayers of Daniel and his companions, the divine solicitude of Joseph betrayed and sold by his brothers. It was David who declared in Psalms 34:6, " *When a poor man cried, and the LORD heard him, and saved him out of all his troubles.*" Or: *"I was glad when they said unto me, let us go into the house of the LORD."* (Psalms 122:1), or *"one thing have I desired of the Lord, that will I seek after; that I may dwell in the house of the Lord all the days of my life ..."* (Psalm 27:4). You can also read Psalms 23:6, Psalm 84:5.

In summary, when considering the **Old Testament**, it is worth noting the establishment of **seven major church periods** that span over a number of centuries. God began and pursued His unique objective, that of spending time with His creatures.

1. In the early church, God is the pastor and the faithful are Adam and Eve.

2. The second period covers the time of Enoch until the time of Noah that represents the second largest church.

3. The third time God went looking for Abram, He changed his name to Abraham and promised to make him the father of a great nation. This encounter between God and Abraham is the third church of Jehovah on earth. It is the church of God with the patriarchs.

4. The fourth period, we see the Creator who went to Moses, convinced him to go with his brother Aaron to deliver the people of Israel from slavery in Egypt. The ministry of Moses for the people of Israel ends at the entrance to Canaan. This is the fourth church. It is the church of the desert.

5. The fifth epoch shows Joshua taking the people of the desert and guiding them to the promised land that was flowing with milk and honey. This is the fifth church, the church of Canaan.

6. The sixth time is the time of the judges, priests and prophets. This is the sixth or theocratic church.

7. The seventh epoch marks the end of the theocratic rule. A monarchy is illustrated by the construction of Solomon's temple, which will mark the climax of the story of the people of Israel. This period is also marked by the rejection of God as King and will result in the destruction of the temple, the captivity and the formal rejection of the Messiah, and the dispersion of the Jewish nation throughout the earth.

Parallel with the seven churches from Revelations.

Just as the 12 Apostles can represent the 12 tribute to Israel (Matthew 19:28, Luke 22:30), It is worthwhile to ask if these seven major periods of the church of the Old Testament are not reproduced in the **New Testament,** especially in **Revelations 1 and 2**. Indeed, the first two chapters of the book of Revelations describe the seven churches of the Christian era — after the passage of Jesus Christ on this earth — and their characteristics, struggles, challenges, weakness, and victories. ***Note that these seven churches do not represent seven separate and independent churches, but rather a continuation of the universal Church at different times in history.*** Therefore we can declare that the church began in the Garden of Eden, with God as shepherd and Adam and Eve as members. Through time, it made its course, continued its mission and will ultimately lead to the universal church when Jesus, once again, will become the ultimate teacher of those who are saved in the restored Eden.

The Church In The New Testament Era

Jesus lays the foundation of his Church

The birth of the Messiah and the establishment of the Christian era open the New Testament. Jesus Christ was presented in the temple according to LUKE 2:21-24. He went there regularly, according to MARK 1:21, and 6:1-6, and MARK 11:27 and 12:35-37, 41-44. He was in the temple at age12 in LUKE 2:41-52; in LUKE 4:15, He taught in the synagogues, and in verse 16, He acted according to his custom, He continued to go to church. According to LUKE 4:31-37, and JOHN 2:13-17, He drove the traders out from the temple saying, *"My house shall be called a house of prayer. But you make it a den of thieves."* He proceeded healed the blind and lame in the temple according to MATTHEW 21:10-17 and MATTHEW 21:23.

Quietly, without pomp, Jesus brought about changes in the attitude of people toward the temple. The Israelites put much emphasis on the Temple, its beauty and meaning. The Temple of Solomon became like the center of their lives, a personal sense of pride. It had a vital importance because it represented the place where God met with His people. Even in the desert, the Lord held a central point and the different tribes were placed around the temporary house of the Lord, so the people had the habit of turning to the temple for everything. The tabernacle and, the sanctuary reflected the presence of God among His children. But notice Jesus' subtle transition:

1. In MATTHEW 24, the disciples wanted to show to Jesus the glory, and the beauty of the building. He replied in verse 2, *"See ye not all these things? Verily I say unto you, there shall not be left here one stone upon another that shall not be thrown down."*

2. When the Samaritan woman told him of places of worship, Jesus said in JOHN 4:21-23, *"the hour has come, when the true worshippers shall worship the Father in spirit and in truth."*

These statements announced a change. The temple was no longer necessarily represented by a physical building. The Jews had lost sight of the main lesson that God wanted to be among them. The difference lies not in the quantity of worshippers or the magnificence of the building where God is worshipped, but instead it is in our relationship with God as He had himself initiated such a relationship in the Garden of Eden.

The purpose of the church is to help people to worship our Maker. The emphasis and focus have always been and must remain God dwelling in us and among us. The apostle Paul would later say in 1 CORINTHIANS 6:19, *"know ye not that your body is the temple of the Holy Ghost."* COLOSSIANS 1:27 says, *"Christ in you, the hope of glory."* Unfortunately, Satan always has his clever counterfeits. To avoid confusion and restore the balance, Jesus had to declare in MATTHEW 18:15-20 that, *"where two or three are gathered together in my name, there am I in the midst of them."* They are worshippers who gather in cells with one accord, to worship God. It is the local church whose major concern is the spiritual beauty of its members. It wants to offer the fragrant bouquet of worship that ascends to God in unity, love and harmony.

In Matthew 16:18, Jesus said *"Upon this rock I will build my church."* Better than anyone else, St. Peter can say which stone Jesus was talking about. He answered in 1 Peter 2:4 by saying *"Come to Jesus, a living stone, rejected by men but chosen and precious to God."* And his counterpart Paul outbid Ephesians 2:20 *"Jesus Christ himself being the Chief cornerstone"*. David had prophesied against the unbelievers in Psalms 118:22, *"The stone which the builders refused is become the head stone of the corner."* Yes! Jesus Christ is the rock upon which the church is built. There are local churches or community-based assemblies. These churches form the universal church against which the gates of hell cannot prevail.

Is the church era still in force?

Based on Revelations 7:9, the ultimate universal church is made up of people from *"all nations, and kindreds, and people, and tongues."* They have one thing in common. They have accepted Jesus Christ as their personal Savior and *"they have washed their robes, and made them white in the blood of the Lamb."* (Revelations 7:14). In other words, Satan will never overwhelm the congregation, the true worshippers of the Almighty, but they will go through tribulation, great tribulation.

Revelations 22:16, says, *"I Jesus have sent mine angel to testify unto you these things in the churches. I am the root and the offspring of David, and the bright and morning star."* Verse 20 says, *"He who testifies these things saith, surely I come quickly. Amen, come, Lord Jesus."*

Taking into account the statements of Jesus that the *"gates of hell shall not prevail against it"* (MATTHEW 16:18). He continues in ordering us to go and preach throughout the world, baptize and teach according to MATTHEW 28:19, 20. I can say confidently that the era of the church will continue until the return of Jesus when he comes to get all the members of the local churches — who form the universal church — to introduce them into God's kingdom and seal everyone's fate. We must preach, baptize and teach until the end. After you and I preach the gospel, new souls will come and accept the Lord for His everlasting mercy. Where will we gather with them and teach them about God's will? If each one of us gets a huge number of baptized believers to follow Jesus, we need a place to meet and fellowship with them. That place is the church, the congregation of saints in which everyone must use their talents and abilities to serve each other for the edification of the saints, according to the Apostle Paul (1 CORINTHIANS 14:5, 12, 22; EPHESIANS 4:12). This will continue until the end of this unjust world. The real dilemma is not the existence of the church, but rather its role and definition. It is not a commercial enterprise, or a ring or a gathering for the most talented and intelligent. Men can change the calendar, use marketing tricks to attract the crowd, and reduce the standard of the church — that is their business. The author of the true church knows those who are genuine, real and those who are imitators. This is not surprising, because the Bible says that Satan will disguise himself as an 'angel of light'. In other words, the true worshippers will have their defined mission until Jesus himself comes to find those preachers at their posts giving the message without alteration, even if only to serve as witnesses. Unfortunately, many tend to add to or subtract from the Gospel. That is the role of triage and screening. One must have God's spirit to distinguish truth from lies. The church of the Master has to be ready and irreproachable. The Almighty will return to pick a glorious church, without spot or wrinkle or blemish (EPHESIANS 5:27). Satan, knowing it, has resorted to all sorts of subterfuge. But regardless of what he may try, the Lord is in control.

The Church at the time of the Apostles.

What can the time of the apostles teach us? ACTS 2:47 tells us that Jesus himself added those who were saved to the church daily. In other words, even after the ascension of the Master, he was paying enough attention to the church body to add unto it those who were saved. The leaders would gather to preach, teach, train and strengthen their faith by word and example. Jesus sent in each local assembly those who were saved, whether it was in Jerusalem, Judea, Antioch, Ephesus, Corinth, Macedonia, Thessalonica, Syria, Cilicia, Galatia, Asia, and everywhere.

When the Apostle Paul had his first encounter with the Lord on the road to Damascus in ACTS 9, he could have told him, *"My dear son I choose you to go to the Gentiles. Make your way and I'll tell you how to open other churches. Stay alone and apart from the others, I'm with you."* No! Jesus sent Paul to the people of the same church that he was persecuting for his initiation as an Apostle. He made the journey with the other Apostles. In JOHN 17:20 Jesus said, *"Neither pray I for these alone, but for them also which shall believe on me through their word."* "

"And other sheep I have, which are not of this fold: them also I must bring, and they shall hear my voice; and there shall be one fold, and one shepherd," JOHN 10:16. During these periods, false brethren and false prophets always existed. The apostles had to confront this issue in most of the churches. Consult their writings in the New Testament and you will be convinced easily of such prevalent situation. Jesus who could see the end from the beginning asked this pertinent question, *"When the son of man cometh, shall he find faith on earth?"* (LUKE 18:8).

Is the Church a perfect body?

The idea that the era of the church is completely gone while we are still living on this earth and short of the great tribulation is not biblical. Every scholar knows that according to Jesus teachings, the church will be dispersed under severe persecution, then the Lord will come to save his people. Jesus continued in MATTHEW 20:16, "*The last shall be first, and the first last.*" MATTHEW 22:14 "*... many are called, but few are chosen.*" When we read MATTHEW 24:11 and 24, Jesus states clearly that many false prophets and false Christ's shall rise and shall even perform great signs and wonders. So true believers, beware. In MATTHEW 24, the Master took great care to warn his followers about three key things:

1. Gave signs that will precede His second coming

2. Warned about the rise of false Christs and false prophets that shall perform great signs and wonders.

3. Mentioned the advent of "*... great tribulation, such as was not since the beginning of the world to this time, no, nor ever shall be.*"

Then in MATTHEW 24:29, 30, he states clearly, "*immediately after tribulation of those days.*" He went on to describe his return. His return shall occur immediately after the great tribulation that no one ever saw before and no one will ever see after.

What does 'Great Tribulation' mean?

To better understand this concept of 'great tribulation', it is advisable to consult the past history which reveals that during the first few centuries AD, the doctrine of Christianity took an extraordinary leap and expanded rapidly. Such a progress triggered a rise to persecution by the Jews, pagans, Roman emperors, local authorities and sometimes even caused the uprising of the general local population. No one can ignore the suffering imposed by Nero, Domitian, Trajan, Hadrian and Antoninus, Marcus Aurelius, Septimius Severus, Maximin the Thracian, Decius, Valerian, Aurelian, Diocletian and Maximian ... The years of cruel torture, however, could not weaken the Christian community. "*The blood of Christians is a seed*", said Tertullian. But the persecution of Christians by Christians was a veritable scourge. After the conversion of Emperor Constantine to Christianity, he published the Edict of Milan in 313 to grant freedom of worship for Christians. But when some Christian churches got to be big, when they were strengthened, they soon wanted to ensure that all followers were subject to their points of doctrine. When some believers dared to question or criticize certain practices of their religions, they were accused of heresy, told to comply or to suffer all sorts of cruelties. To cite as evidence, note the persecution of the Albigenses, the Huguenots, against Protestantism, and the practice of the Inquisition.

Among the tortures of the past, we can mention: being eaten by dogs, people tied to stakes with tunics soaked with resin and sulfur for use as lighting for night games in the circus, crucifixion, decapitation, delivered to wild beasts, the flames waves, their blood shed here and there, etc. Even nowadays, many countries continue to persecute Christians, sentencing them to death, gang rape, locking them in 'park for Christians' that are unhealthy and unbearable. But the Bible says that when "*the great persecution*" of the last days come around, it will still be worse.

At that time of great tribulation, all 'true believers' will be severely persecuted. They will no longer be able to gather together in regular assembly because the devil will use the worldly system to go after the "*true Christians*" (REVELATIONS 16:14). The devil will take over the worldly system to make it go after the true believers, accusing them of being the cause of all the woes, catastrophes and disaster on earth, as described in the book of REVELATIONS, including chapters 16 and 18. The devil will try to annihilate all sincere believers who put their trust in God alone and are saved by grace through Jesus Christ. They will no longer be able to gather in groups, as churches. Therefore the physical authentic churches will automatically collapse while other churches will seem to be flourishing. Remember REVELATIONS 13:14, and MATTHEW 7:21-23. This will be the end of the church era because, according to MATTHEW 24 verse 29, 30, "*And then shall appear the sign of the Son of man in heaven."* This may be hard to believe, but consult history, and remember the persecutions, inquisitions, crusades in the past. They were led mostly by believers against believers. Toward the end of time, when Jesus is about to return to this earth, they will happen again. They will definitely be even worse. Read MATTHEW 24:21, and REVELATIONS 12:17.

Certainly, the church often has stepped out of the norm of true followers of the Almighty, and missed the marks set by Jesus Christ and his disciples. But if and when it goes astray, it must be told and proven so. It must repent, confess its sins, humble itself and seek God's favor not by meritorious works, but by prayer, humility and supplication to the Creator so that he can have mercy on those who beg for forgiveness. Lately, the devil has been able to be successful in luring people into believing that 'everything is all right'. God will save you all. Jesus paid it all. Enjoy life. Even those who claim to have the truth, or might have had it at one time, but through laziness, have lost it, but are still convinced they have it.

It is really unbecoming and disheartening to hear people talking about the end of the church era and encouraging the faithful to divert the money to them for their personal ministries. This is hypocrisy. You cannot want to destroy a biblical system and replace it with a human fabrication, based on your own dreams, illuminations and speculations. Anathema! Woe unto those who lead God's people into error. Woe to those who let the spirit of delusion seize them for believing lies. Again, according to the Bible, the church will continue to exist until that time of great tribulation that is coming sooner than most of us think. The church is the meeting place for faithful worshippers to worship their Lord. Jesus spoke of two or three worshipers. He is not concerned about the quantity. He is not going to bend his principles to average out and save as many as he possibly can. On the other hand, he will not cast out those who come to him and accept his free offer of salvation. What should we do when others arrive? Should we drive them away, tell them no more than two or three? There will be gatherings and assemblies until the new heaven and new earth come. The key question is, for what purpose? Who are they really worshipping?

It is worthwhile to examine our position vis-à-vis the church's philosophy and the speculation surrounding its existence. We must be careful not to err in either extreme.

Is The Era of God's Church Over?

According to a German proverb, *"In every man there is a bit of all men."* Therefore everything that requires the presence of mankind reflects the characteristics of all humans. We know that we have short-comings and defects; therefore our actions and businesses reflect a tapestry of imperfection. Some believe it should be different for believers. The people of the church should be perfect. Given the objectionable conduct of those who claim to be Christians, the observers are so shocked and outraged that they question the purpose of the Church and even the necessity of its existence. This cry has become increasingly popular and, even among those who attend religious congregations. For them, the religious man should have been above all reproach. Since it is otherwise, why continue with religion? Some representatives of religion even dare to preach that the church age is over, give the exact date when the church era ended and proceed to specify the month, day and year for the end of the world. Let us consult the Holy Words. Throughout the ages, there have always been people devoid of any insight who love to take a few verses from the Bible, and claim to have received the last lights, or the ultimate revelation from High above, and begin to proclaim a gospel that disappoints and confuse many.

According to **Isaiah 8:20, everything we say must pass through the filter of sacred law and testimony. If not, and we are all sailing in the dark on a stormy sea. *"Ye shall know them by their fruits,"* said Jesus in**

MATTHEW 7:16. Others, a bit confused, wonder what the role of Christianity is in the post-modern society. When they see the sensational news coming from the media, many are convinced that the church is full of scandalous stories of: murder, robbery, sexual abuse, pedophilia, prevarication, power struggles, jealousies and gossip. Some wonder if today's church is administered directly by Satan. Why not get rid of the institution to expose those hiding behind religion to advance their own agendas? Others proclaim loudly that the era of the church has ended definitely. They have become allergic to the word '**church**'. For true believers, they must be able to put aside all the emotions and noise to take the time to consult the Bible.

Difference between religion and church.

There is a difference between **religion** that deals with people's beliefs and the attitudes toward the existence of super natural beings and deities and the **church** that has to deal with the assembly of believers. In this book, church is a universal congregation of Christians, worshippers of God.

It includes people from all walks of life who are characterized by these basic steps:

1. Admit one's sinful nature.

2. Realize that sin leads to death.

3. Realize one's inability to get rid of the sinful condition.

4. Accepting Christ as the sole source of salvation.

5. Persevere in the faith while taking care of others

According to ACTS 17:11, it is necessary to examine the scriptures daily to determine if what people are saying about the church's role is true. In light of scripture, why not try to see what is right?

According to Psalms 8 and 19, all creation tells of the glory of God who favorably receives praises and thanks from his creatures through his church.

Evolution of the church through time.

The church is, by definition, an assembly of believers who share the same faith, have the same mission, and are committed to improving the human condition, in all areas, by all means and conditions. The role of the church is considered on three levels:

1. The local church.
2. The local community, and
3. The historic Church.

These assemblies began with the early church and the universal Church, and grew throughout the ages. Nevertheless, there is a designated place where believers can encounter their Creator. We can define it as the elected assembly of God (eklesia), saved by the blood of Jesus. ISAIAH 6:1-3 describes a scene in which, *"the Lord sitting upon a throne, high and lifted up, and his train filled the temple. Seraphims stood above it: each one had six wings … and one cried unto another, and said, "Holy, holy holy is the Lord of hosts. The whole earth is full of his glory'."*

It appears from these statements that the Master of the Universe plays an active role on this earth and focuses his attention on human activities.

Attitudes within the Church.

Everyone who belongs to the church must examine their attitude, and be aware that the church itself can cause us to stumble.

Let us avoid the extremes.

All extremes fall short from the intended goal.

a.) The first extreme — salvation through the church only — goes back to very ancient times. Man stands as spiritual leader of the church, and wants to control his fellow men. He may forget he is working under the ultimate Ruler. It is sad, but to be frank, often religion is the preferred way for man to operate, exploit, manipulate and dominate his fellow men. And then, present the church as the only means of salvation. *"Extra Ecclesiam, nulla salus."* (Outside of the church, there is no salvation). This is the philosophy adopted by the zealots since the 2nd century, preaching that the church is the only means of salvation. So for these leaders, the church plays a role of co-redeemer. ***Many believe there are three conditions for salvation:***

1. The Blessed Virgin.
2. The Church.
3. Jesus.

If that is a beautiful, and even a romantic theory, it is not biblical. Indeed, in Acts 4:12 we read, *"There is no other name under heaven given among men, whereby we must be saved."*

Contrary to paganism, there is only one God and only on mediator:

Jesus Christ, the Lord.

While Jesus was on this earth, there were people who already wanted to deify Mary, to put her as a gate keeper for salvation. In Luke 11:27, 28 *"And it came to pass, as he spake these things, a certain woman of the company lifted up her voice, and said unto him,* ***Blessed*** *is the womb that bare thee, and the paps which thou hast sucked. But Jesus said, Yea rather, blessed are they that hear the word of God, and keep it"*. Jesus' answer indicates clearly that He does not condone such an idea. Jesus wanted to emphasize the fact that salvation is through him alone. Everyone who hears God's word and obeys it is blessed through His unique sacrifice. Jesus himself had to say according to John 14:6, *"I am the way, the truth, and the life: No man comes unto the Father, but by me."* It is a radical and categorical statement. When a church boasts of being the only guardian of true Christianity, we must wonder and become weary. Protestants responded, and protested. They said 'Sola Scriptura!' 'Sola Fide'. Those who followed the evolution of facts established that shortly thereafter, to ensure that everyone stayed in the same denomination, the Protestant churches started using the same approach, namely, salvation through their organization, if only in a more flexible or subtle manner. Today, every religious denomination says: *"My movement, my church, my organization represent the sole holder of the truth, the only one to lead you to salvation"*.

When the 'Laodicean' church came, it started very well, but it is time for that church to review and meditate upon this word found in Revelations 3:17

"Because thou sayest, I am rich, and increased with goods, and have need of nothing; and knowest not that thou art wretched, and miserable, and poor, and blind, and naked."

These words seem to evoke an attitude problem. A church may have the truth, may preach the right doctrine and have everything, but lack the main thing, a total surrender to Jesus, a unique and very close relationship with the Master. Beloved, when people see us, do they see Jesus? Or do they see stuck up and self righteous people who know they have the true doctrine that saves? If only Jesus saves, then we can prove we accept such a salvation by faith by producing the fruits that are worth the heavenly calling. We must be careful not to mouth the same trumpet, 'out of my organization, no salvation.' We may never say it but we may behave like it. Such an approach is somewhat biased. Only Jesus can save. It has never been otherwise. ISAIAH 45:17 states that *"Israel shall be saved in the Lord with an everlasting salvation."* REVELATIONS 19:1 says, *"And after these things I heard a great voice of much people in heaven, saying, Alleluia; Salvation and glory, and honor, and power, unto the Lord our God." "He became the author of eternal salvation unto all them that obey him."* (HEBREWS 5:9).

b.) The other extreme is the total rejection of the church. Because of too many scandals, too much profanity, and too much bluff, Satan is running the church, so let's get rid of it. Its time is over. This is the post church era. Not so fast, brethren. Note that constructing, consolidating the church, since the Garden of Eden, has always provoked an antipathic reaction on the part of Satan. This is illustrated by the different scandals. There was an uproar in the garden, scandals in the time of Noah, Abraham, Moses, Joshua, judges and priests, Solomon … When Jesus came to this earth, he declared, *"It must be that scandals offenses come, but woe to that man by whom the offense cometh."* "And then shall many be offended, and shall betray one another, and shall hate one another. And many false prophets shall rise, and shall deceive many. And because iniquity shall abound, the love of many shall wax cold. But he that shall endure unto the end, the same shall be saved." (MATTHEW 24:10-13). MATTHEW 24:24 says *"There shall arise false Christs and false prophets, they will show great signs and miracles to deceive if possible even the elect."*

c.) Satan, very astute and manages to get a third category under his control. It consists of those who know that the blood of Jesus Christ provides salvation by grace. All they need to do is to accept it by faith. But they go a step further: Jesus paid it all so they develop a false sense of permanent salvation without any true and sincere progress in their relation with the Almighty. Let us recall the statement of the apostle Paul in 1 CORINTHIANS 9:27, *"But I keep under my body, and bring it into subjection: lest that by any means, when I have preached to others, I myself should be a castaway"*

In PHILIPPIANS 2:12 Paul says *"Wherefore, my beloved, as ye have always obeyed, not as in my presence only, but now much more in my absence, work out your own salvation with fear and trembling."* This does not mean we can earn salvation through our deeds, but we must stay on the ball and persevere. In this group there are those who feel they are righteous, they are justified because they are the only ones to meet all the criteria for eternal life. The Most High warns us by the prophet Jeremiah. JEREMIAH 9:23, 24 *"Thus saith the LORD, Let not the wise man glory in his wisdom, neither let the mighty man glory in his might, let not the rich man glory in his riches: But let him that glorieth glory in this, that he understandeth and knoweth me, that I am the LORD which exercise loving kindness, judgment, and righteousness, in the earth: for in these things I delight, saith the LORD."*

Beloved these positions do not give us the solution. They welcome the common enemy who wins, whether it is salvation through the church or without the church, or without true submission to Christ. Remember what Jesus told Nicodemus in JOHN 3:3, *"You must be born again."* What really counts once we accept God's grace is our degree of intimacy and our relationship with Him. The church can help you but it can also turn you away from Jesus if — once you belong to it — you become self righteous and develop a false sense of permanent salvation and if you forget that the sole purpose of the church is to prepare souls for the eternal kingdom. 2 PETER 3:18 says, *"Grow in grace, and in the knowledge of our Lord and Savior Jesus Christ. To him be glory both now and forever. Amen."*

ROMANS 3:31 says, *"Do we make void the law through faith? God forbid: yea, we establish the law."* As for our salvation, it is a relational matter of every soul with God. The church is like a bus that sits all passengers who have the same, single destination. We must have our eyes wide open for setbacks and detours. Sometimes, if the bus breaks down or loses its direction, we must repair it, re direct it, arrange to leave and make sure we take the one that will achieve the desired destination and get us to the right station safely. The church allows us to preach to others so that together, all of us can be ready to meet Jesus. When you see that the church is a subject of stress, worries, persecution, humiliation, betrayal, hypocrisy, pride, and politics, we must be careful not to give the enemy an opportunity to overcome us, discourage us or make us bitter. Some situations can threaten our everlasting salvation. Do not be too emotionally attached to a particular building or leader. Be only closely linked with the Lord, the ultimate Savior.

In GALATIANS 5:15 Paul says, "... *if you bite and devour one another, take heed that you be not consumed one of another.*" It continues in verse 16 saying, "*Walk in the Spirit, and you shall not fulfill the lust of the flesh.*" These desires of the flesh are clearly elucidated in verses 19-21: fornication, uncleanness, lasciviousness, idolatry, witchcraft, hatred, contentions, jealousies, animosities, quarrels, divisions, sects, envy, drunkenness, and orgies. You can easily add hypocrisy, the clan spirit, the spirit of revenge, manipulation, slander, vanity, pride, selfishness, perjury, treason, animosity, rebellion, and other works of the flesh. In these 21st century, temptations of the flesh are more pronounced. The moral decay seems to condone such behavior. It is very challenging, almost impossible to keep a clean spirit when you are constantly bombarded by all possible means by things to foster lust and covetousness. Those who perform the works of the flesh will not inherit the kingdom of heaven, so a church that excels through such undesirable traits and actions is heading straight to perdition. Beware flock of sheep. Do not follow a multitude to do evil, according to EXODUS 23:2. It is difficult, but in Christ, life can take a different course. It may not be perfect, but let us not get discouraged. We must never give up. If we fall, by God's grace, we get up and march on. All of us want to have eternal life. Then GALATIANS 5:25 says, *"If we live in the Spirit, let us also walk in the Spirit."*

Summary.

To summarize: God did not start the church to allow some to ensure their hegemony in preaching their own gospel. Let us remember, in the spiritual realm, 99.999999% of truth is still considered lying to God. This means God wants complete obedience, no turning back, and no holding back. Sin is a cancer. No one would feel comfortable knowing there is a cancerous spot in his lung or brain. It is the same for sin. We must examine everything we hear or are taught. Be cautious and ask God for the spirit of discernment so we are not distracted from the right track. God has not rejected his Church in its entirety. By the same token, He will not automatically save people just because of their association to a pastor, denomination, or church. It is not about obeying the majority rules or laws. It is not a question of whether or not everybody is doing it, then it must be right. It must be according to God's words in the Bible. Some churches will perish with their members and their leaders. Others will receive eternal rewards for accepting the salvation offered free for maintaining a dynamic relationship with Jesus Christ, who will save his universal church, which must be spotless. Beware of the fact that the devil is at work in more subtle ways than we can imagine. The church has lost its good habits, zeal, and zest to work for God's kingdom. Its attention is often turned toward capitalism, making money, getting popular, accommodating great contributors, being politically correct and making a lot of noise. In the process, it has forgotten its mission. It has switched its priorities illustrated with what I call the three 'P':

1. Popularity.

2. Prosperity

3. Power in this secular world.

The apostle John warns us in 1 John 2:15, *"Love not the world, neither the things that are in the world. If any man loves the world, the love of the Father is not in him."* To have ignored these eternal truths, the church has become a patchwork full of contradiction. The result is astounding. It has become a lucrative business and in many cases, a springboard for many to pursue their petty agendas. Therefore, it is not surprising to see the meetings filled with people who do not know the true God. The tares are swarming everywhere and seem to be smothering the good grain.

But God has never lost control of his true church.

Six key reasons why the church age is not over.

1. Lucifer is God's creature. He was very beautiful. He was called 'son of the morning'. Nevertheless he was and is a creature. As a general rule, the creature is not stronger than the Creator. Lucifer revolted against the Almighty, he lost big time. Read Isaiah 14:12-14, Ezekiel 28:17, and Revelations 12:7-12. According to Genesis 3:15, his defeat was forecasted in the Garden of Eden. He lost to Jesus when He was on the earth, according to Matthew 4:1-9. Ultimately Satan will be destroyed forever. Revelation 19:19, 20 (he is cast alive into a lake of fire burning with brimstone). For God to let the devil take over his church at this time, like some are saying, would be conceding to the devil. Is this possible? No!

2. Satan has declared an open war to God's remnant church. He wants to destroy it. REVELATIONS 12:17 says, "*The dragon was wroth with the woman (the church), and went to make war with the remnant of her seed, which keep the Commandments of God, and have the testimony of Jesus Christ.*" Jesus loves his church so much, he died for it. He gives his relationship with the church as an illustration as to how a couple should love one another, "*Husbands, love your wives, even as Christ also loved the church, and gave himself for it*", (EPHESIANS 5:21-33). If Jesus can reach a point where he is so fed up with his beloved church that he can no longer deal with it and gives it up to the devil, then all husbands in the world can use the same argument and do the same. If that were true, man would have used that excuse most of the time. Jesus is the supreme head of the church (EPHESIANS 1:22,23). If he abandons it, a 'decapitated body' is a dead body. But through Paul, he calls his church, "*the church of the living God, the pillar and ground of the truth*" (1 TIMOTHY 3:15). Do you think God would just give up and hand the church over to Satan? No way!

3. MATTHEW 16:18 says, "*the gates of hell shall not prevail against it.*" After making such a statement, how can God change his mind and hand the church over to the prime candidate for hell, Satan? No! According to MATTHEW 25, hell is reserved for the devil and his angels.

4. The church has sacred duties:

a. Preaching the gospel until the end of this world (MATTHEW 28:18-20), *b.* Baptizing those who believe (1 CORINTHIANS 12:13; MATTHEW 16:16),

c. Ministering to the needs of the believers one another, (GALATIANS 5:13, 1 CORINTHIANS 12:1-28),

d. Praying for the sick (JAMES 5:14-16), and

e. Participating in the washing of feet (JOHN 13:1-17), and holy Communion (1 CORINTHIANS 10:15, 16, and 11:22-28).

Did God give up on those ministries after he participated in them? No!

5. The Lord takes those who are saved and add them to the CHURCH ACTS 2:47 *"And the Lord added to the church daily such as should be saved."* Has he found another secret place to keep them until he comes back? No!

6. After our first parents disobeyed God's command and sinned, there have been two camps of people: a multitude who follow their own will and desire and some who have chosen to stay faithful to his word. As time goes by, the number of rebellious people increases, from Cain versus Abel to the multitude during the flood, and on and on. God always has true believers on this earth. He is not about to change at the last minute. You shall have trials and tribulations but be of good faith, said Jesus. Abel chose to serve the Lord, and Noah, Henoch, Abraham, Joseph, Moses, Daniel and his companions, The Albigeois, Vaudois, Huguenots, John Wycliffe, Luther, Jean Hus, etc., all chose to serve the Lord with their own free will. At no point in time

did God say, 'the earth is too wicked let me isolate, shield my true believers'. None of them went into a secret place, inside a compound, on top of a mountain to sing, fast and pray constantly. They remain connected to God. Jesus, God's son, could have showed up for a few days, causes some stir with his message, arranged to be condemned and crucified, and finish the work quickly in a week or so. However, he was born and he grew up among men but stayed focus on his mission. In John 17:15, Jesus specifically states, *"I pray not that thou shouldest take them out of the world, but that thou shouldest keep them from the evil"*. Therefore, the arguments that the world is too wicked, the church is corrupted, God had to close it, are not fool proof. To the contrary, many texts speak about the last days, including Daniel 12:1 and Mark 13:19, 24. Matthew 24:21, 22 mentions days of great tribulation. *"Except those days should be shortened, there should no flesh be saved: but for the elect's sake those days shall be shortened."* There will be a time of great persecution when calamities fall on this earth, and the true believers will be blamed and persecuted.

We are getting closer, and all true believers can feel it already. Freedom, security, and stability are becoming more fragile. Extremists are terrorizing the world in the name of misguided religious beliefs. The free world seems to be at the mercy of a few extremists in the name of religion. Soon the secular world will get suspicious of every religion. Sincere believers will be identified through trials and tribulations. According to Matthew 24:24, *"If it were possible, even the very elect could have been deceived."* This will be moving toward the end of the great controversy between God and evil.

True believers already know who the ultimate victor is — those who have remained faithful.

Remember the saying, 'it is darkest before dawn'. Because the church is the object of Satan's wrath, he is fighting against it at all angles, and using all kinds of ways to weaken the church, such as false doctrine, sophisticated theology/philosophy, the complacence of its members, a false sense of secured salvation, being stuck up, division, discord, hypocrisy, scandalous behavior among brethren and even spiritual leaders, administrative tactics, manipulating techniques, persecution by authorities, principalities, spiritual wickedness in high places, and many others. This is why, the Apostle Paul challenges the church members to put on the whole armor of God. Check it out in Ephesians 6:11-18, *"Put on the whole armor of God, that ye may be able to stand against the wiles of the devil. For we wrestle not against flesh and blood, but against principalities, against powers, against the rulers of the darkness of this world, against spiritual wickedness in high places. Therefore take unto you the whole armor of God, that ye may be able to withstand in the evil day, and having done all, to stand. Stand therefore, having your loins girt about with truth, and having on the breastplate of righteousness; and your feet shod with the preparation of the gospel of peace; above all, taking the shield of faith, wherewith ye shall be able to quench all the fiery darts of the wicked. And take the helmet of salvation, and the sword of the Spirit, which is the word of God: Praying always with all prayer and supplication in the Spirit, and watching thereunto with all perseverance and supplication for all saints."* Let us use it!

When is Jesus really returning on this earth?

Do we know the date on which Christ will return to take all of us with him to introduce us to everlasting happiness and joy? We live in an age when many are inclined to say that the return of Jesus is near and at the door. Many signs of the times are being fulfilled, the prophecies are coming true. It is clear that the return of the Master is closer than ever before. People want to know the date. From the time when Jesus was on earth, his disciples also were being consumed by the desire to know this fateful date. The master replied: when it comes to the day and hour no one knows, (MATTHEW 24:36). Nevertheless, some people are convinced that they know the exact date of Christ's return on this earth. To support their claims, they cite a few texts in the Bible. My Bible reveals that because of the wickedness of mankind, Noah was asked to build an Arch, then the flood came. Noah was not given detailed date regarding the beginning and the end of the flood, (Genesis 6,7 and 8). Jonah was toll to the people of Nineveh that in 40 days the entire city will be overthrown. Now, when did those 40 days begin? Was it when Jonah decided to flee from the Lord, or was it when the fish vomited out Jonah upon the dry land, or was it when he started preaching, or was it when the word finally reached the King and preparations were being made to fast and pray? Jonah did not have such a privilege to know the exact time. Did the number forty simply meant a period of probation, trial and chastisement as it tends to be universally interpreted. Could it be that God used the number forty for the Nineveh because, in his omniscience, he foresaw grace (number 5), revival and renewal (number 8) for those inhabitants of that great city? Again, Only God knows. **No human being can read God's clock. None can reach over God's shoulder to see his writings.** The true Christian must always be ready because if he or she passes from life to death, his/her eternal destiny is decided. 2 JOHN 9 and 10 states that anyone who goes beyond the doctrine of Christ is a transgressor, and God is not with him. One should not even say hello to such a person. Beware! Christ gave us many signs and told us to be on our guard, to preach the gospel, to watch and pray. Personally, I believe the Lord is around the corner. "*Soon, and very soon we are going to see the LORD.*" But only God knows the exact date. As for me, I know one thing, I must be ready. That's good enough for me. What about you? *"Brothers, what shall we do?"* Be ready to receive the Master whatever the day and hour of his return in glory. In the interim, should we continue to attend church?

Should We Still Go To Church?

Scientific discoveries and technology continue to advance over the years with higher expectations for a much better world. Their impact is felt in all areas, including religion, but not for the best. Therefore, is it not surprising to see a change in attitude even among the most devout believers. Some people want to continue with the beliefs and traditions of the past, while others dare to question the role of religion in their lives. Some even put the church on the backburner when faced with emergencies, personal and community challenges. For them, conventional responses inspired by old biblical cases are not relevant enough to solve the pressing issues facing the new generations of this century and beyond. We also find that many who claim to be believers, if they have not abandoned their faith altogether, have become lukewarm, tend to get less involved in ecclesial activities and choose to remain at home at the usual hours of church service. Some numb their conscience by watching a televised worship of their choice. Others visit various meetings here and there, but without any personal commitment to a local, or a specific congregation. A final category eventually abandons the faith and blames the leaders, their parents, or the system in general. According to Exodus 34:7, the eternal God does not mistake the innocent for the guilty.

Why do some drop out of church?

If you ask why these people have changed their spiritual attitude, they will say, perhaps:

a.) The service is bland, unattractive and archaic, it lacks authenticity and does not reflect the practical life.

b.) Most religious leaders are hypocrites, or greedy. Church members have no life in them. The church does not distinguish itself from the crowd. It is not genuine.

c.) The message preached is often meaningless, or negative, with a tendency to blame the faithful or pacify them. It brings them to resignation. It wants them to accept the status quo. Sometimes, people even feel they are responsible for the unfortunate circumstances of their existence. It is the reward for evil deeds committed in private or in public by themselves or previous generations.

d.) The bad propaganda surrounding the era of the church as we have seen lately.

It is obvious that sometimes religion in general or Christianity in particular, goes through moments of crisis. A general trend of doubt and questioning may even shake the church and force it to move to a higher level. Lately the challenges seem so overwhelming in this secular world that many are wondering and asking questions.

Should we continue to go to church: yes or no? Why?

Once again, it is worth to state unequivocally that attending any religious organizations does not appear in the Bible as a prerequisite for eternal life. Moreover, for Christians, only Jesus can give free access to the eternal kingdom by his grace. This is why it is very important to follow his examples. Attending church regularly can have a positive impact on and benefit the life of every believer. The presence of a believer in a congregation can be beneficial for two reasons.

I. A spiritual impact

II. A socio-cultural impact

I — Spiritual Impact

a.) The first reason why believers are invited to join a church is because God wants the same for the spiritual growth and welfare of his children. In fact the Bible says that the Creator takes pleasure in meeting people and to share their company. *"Mine house shall be called a house of prayer for all people."* (ISAIAH 56:7). It is also a sign whereby the believer shows his love for his Creator and his submission to his will according to 1 CORINTHIANS 1:9. It is God's will. It pleases him. He makes ample provision for us to be spiritually fed. The Bible mentions several examples:

PSALM 50:5, 23, *"Gather to me my faithful, who made a covenant with me by sacrifice! Anyone who offers sacrifice of thanksgiving glorifies me, and he who guards his way will see the salvation of God."*

PSALM 122:1, *"I was glad when they said unto me, let us go into the house of the LORD."*

PSALM 84:2, 5, *"My soul longs and faints for the courts of the Lord. Blessed are they that dwell in thy house: they will be still praising thee."* According to ACTS 2:47, the Lord leads those who are saved to the church. If God had a better place to guide those who have accepted to serve him, certainly he would have done so. Remember, Jesus himself set the example when he was on this earth by going regularly to synagogue. (Read MARK 1:21,

6:1-6, MARK 11: 27;12 :35-37, 41-44. It is in the temple at 12 years, LUKE 2:41-52; In LUKE 4:14, he taught in the synagogues, in verse 16, he acts according to his custom, he continues to do according to LUKE 4:31-37).

b.) It is a means to demonstrate and engage in the exercises of piety include, praying for each other, fasting, teaching, listening, learning, exhorting, offering and tithing with the main focus on God, our benefactor, and not by customs, routine or man-made burdens. PSALMS 133:1,3 says, *"Here, oh, it is pleasant, it is for brethren to dwell together in unity! … This is where the Lord commanded the blessing, life for eternity."*

c.) The church is a means to strengthen our faith by listening to the exhortations, testimonies and successes of one another and helping each other in our daily struggles. ROMANS 10:17 says, *"faith comes by hearing and hearing by the word of God."* For us to grow in Christ there must be the proper teaching, and learning .

d.) It is an opportunity for the mind to accommodate and engage in different type of activity. Such a change allows the mind to appreciate a variety in thoughts and priorities. In fact, throughout the week we have to deal with all kinds of problems from work, home, traveling, navigating through peaks and valleys of the mundane life, and personal discomfort. When the day and time come to go to church, we should experience relief. For at least a few hours, we can forget about our problems or hand them over to God with prayers and supplications, focus on a great Father and the wonders of his creation. 2 PETER 3:18 says, *"Grow in the grace and knowledge of our Lord and Savior Jesus Christ."*

e.) It is an opportunity to exhort each other and care for one another. 2 TIMOTHY 3:3-9 cites among the signs of the last days, men shall be lovers of themselves, covetous, and boasters. They only want to satisfy themselves. They want to enjoy life, and are lovers of pleasures, sometime even at the expense of their neighbors, without regard for those around them, but they have no real control of their lives or their deaths. In addition, we are bombarded by attacks, philosophies, and a secular realm of logic that denies the existence of God. Therefore, willingly or unwillingly, despite all strategies and rebuttals, such arguments ultimately affect our understanding and thinking about spiritual things. This is why the church requires the presence of spiritual leaders who are competent and eager to guide the flock in the right path. HEBREWS 13:17 says, *"Obey them that have the rule over you, and submit yourselves: for they watch for your souls, as they that must give account, that they may do it with joy, and not with grief: for that is unprofitable for you."* 1 JOHN 1:3 *"What we have seen and heard declare we unto you, that ye also may have fellowship with us: and truly our fellowship is with the Father, and with his Son Jesus Christ."*

II — Socio-cultural

Attendance to a church allows us to meet great needs such as:

a.) Our need to belong to a group, 'No man is an island'. According to the socio-cultural models, we need to belong to a family, and a community in order to function at our full potential in all areas of life. When everyone in a community shares the same goal, the combined effort of the members of a community has a significant and positive impact on all the members of the community collectively and individually. In Matthew 18:19, Jesus says, "*if two of you shall agree on earth as touching any thing that they shall ask, it shall be done for them of my father which is in heaven.*"

b.) Every now and then we need a break, a change of activities in order to renew our strength and then resume the journey.

c.) We need protection against boredom and loneliness. Whoever is left alone all the time, sooner or later will wind up at a stand still. No one person alone can possess, process or understand the scope of the whole Bible. We must listen to comments, explanations, exhortations, and the teachings of someone else for new opportunities, and understandings. "*From the clash of ideas light shines.*" and new insights are gained.

d.) We need an objective assessment of ourselves and our performance. The human race has a natural tendency to go easy on itself and become complacent. One can quickly become stagnant, living by pure routine, and may move backward by lack of 'positive competition' without being aware of it. For if we do not listen to other challenges, reflections, or approaches from community members, we may feel satisfied and stay at a plateau early.

e.) We need the support and community spirit to cope with the trials, tribulations, divorce, illness, death, tragedy, economic disaster and family / personal challenges of life. Whatever the faults and defects of our brothers and sisters, it is worth having them to help us turn the tide.

f.) We need to be useful, exercise our talents, and appreciate those of us who share the same faith (music, sports, recreation, games, arts , etc.). The secular world, or those who do not share our faith, may engage in activities that are contrary to our faith. With people who share common interests and aspirations, the number of unpleasant surprises is reduced. How many times is a Christian couple invited to small family gatherings for some private parties, weddings or other celebratory occasions? Then shortly after, the atmosphere changes; It is the haunting music, dance, the use of alcohol and cigarettes. This couple is uncomfortable and must know when to leave. We need to show understanding and to identify deviations, and imitations, along with the discernment to know when to retire or not to attend.

The proper attitude toward the church according to the Bible.

You can browse through the entire Bible, especially the New Testament, but you will not find the custom of separating the faithful, with everyone in his little corner doing his own thing. Some may want to be completely separated from others. But, in Hebrews 10:25 we read, *"not forsaking the assembling of ourselves together, as the manner of some is; but exhorting one another: and so much the more, as ye see the day approaching."* Here the author exhorts believers to remain steadfast in the faith, especially when they see the day approaching. What day does he speak about in the text? The day of Jesus's return. In other words, when we approach the end of time, we must unite, be vigilant, stick together and make sure we are ready to mount guards against all winds of false doctrine attempting to deter us from our ultimate goal. One way to be prepared is to attend church spiritual meetings regularly with the spirit of the Bereans who "*... examined the Scriptures daily to see if what Paul said was true*" (Acts 17:11). This is the obligation of every authentic Christian until the time when the church gathering will no longer be feasible, shortly before Jesus's return. No one can claim to belong to the universal church while remaining fundamentally opposed to the idea of belonging to a local church or a group for fellowship. If the church abandons the right tracks, our role, as its members, is to pray, identify the source of apostasy, pray, exhort and beseech those in charge to take action. If they listen and proper changes occur, then reform is made. If they resist and ignore you, then you need to prepare to abandon this assembly and look at the prospect of finding another congregation that meets the biblical requirements, after earnest prayers. Wherever the apostles went, they would organize a church no matter how small it was. In order to maintain the flame and rekindle the faith of the converts, we need to be involved. For example, see the Acts of the Apostles and those who followed Jesus. This should be enough to convince you.

The church is a body that is well developed. In order to build a given house, all materials, and parts of that house must be collected in one place for a specific habitable house. How relevant is it for someone to state he has a house because he has a blueprint, while none of the walls are placed together? If one wall is in Geneva, another in Washington, D.C., another in Georgia or Paris, another in Port-au-Prince, Haiti, while the roof in Martinique, with the foundation in Japan, can we call that a house? That would be madness.

Of course there are always exceptions such as: cases of illnesses, or if a church is not available where you live, etc.. Being involved in the daily activities of a church allows us to leverage our talents to build the body of Christ. 1 CORINTHIANS 12 claimed the diversity of gifts for the well being of all members of the church so the church should function smoothly as all members of the human body function in unison for the full development of the organism. We attend church to worship the King of Kings, to pray, donate, contribute to the preaching of the gospel, strengthen our faith and to persevere on the path that leads to eternal happiness. We acquire that path only by the atoning blood of our Lord and Savior, Jesus Christ who is the head. The church is the body and we are part of that body, according to 1 CORINTHIANS 12:27.

How To Identify The True Church?

Throughout the earth, and especially in the Western civilization, religious assemblies swarm like wild mushrooms. The number of believers also seems to increase. In some places, without exaggeration, there is at least one church at every intersection. They all profess to be the true church and each of them claims to be the sole owner and holder of the truth. Most of them confess to follow Jesus as their only Savior. Some go so far as to state that only those who are part of their organization have access to eternal salvation. They tend to contradict themselves. To reassure their members, they do not hesitate to condemn all other assemblies that do not belong to their organization, calling them apostate churches, Babylon, or whatever else. If you go and visit the official records of the different religions, they generally have one thing in common-contradiction. Each of them wants us to believe that salvation is only through its organization. Certainly this creates a dilemma for many. It is a chaotic situation. How can so many people claim to have a truth that is unique and universal? Nowhere in the common Bible, and specifically in the New Testament, do we find this antagonistic, competitive, elitist and separatist gospel that seems to tear apart the body of Christ instead of uniting it. In LUKE verses 9:49, 50 we read, *"John answered and said, 'Master, we saw one casting out devils in thy name; and we forbad him, because he followed not with us.' Jesus replied: 'forbid him not: for he that is not against us is for us'."* John's initial reaction showed his lack of knowledge and power, some insecurity and a lack of understanding of the scope of the mission of Jesus Christ. It reflects the natural man's knee jerk reaction when he feels that his territory is being invaded. He tends to be selfish, narrow-minded, bigoted and jealous for his preeminence at the expense of others. This shows a lack of maturity. After all, he who merely preaches Jesus and uses his name only for his own egotistic purposes will eventually disperse.

Who is the founder of the Church?

Since we are talking about the Christian Church, it does not have any other founder but Christ himself. At no time during the term of his earthly life did Jesus give the go-ahead to one person or one single group to have a monopoly or exclusivity in terms of denomination or religious affiliation. However, before he left, Jesus established **his** universal church, based upon a sound doctrine he took years to transmit to his disciples. If we really want to know the truth, we should consult the blue print found in the Holy Bible to identify the true church. Better yet, from the time Jesus left, around two thousand years ago, there has not been a definite rupture of God's activities. God never abandoned his assembly. Speaking to the disciples, we read in JOHN 20:21-23, *"Jesus said to them, Peace be unto you: as my Father has sent me, so I sent you. He breathed on them and said to them: Receive the Holy Spirit."* He gave to all the disciples equal privilege to work in his church. But their impact depends on their individual talents and gifts. All, not Peter alone, received the Holy Spirit to engage in the ministry of God. Note that Jesus founded one Church. He did not endorse the formation of many, if not thousands of churches. He said: "*I will build my*

Church." He is not the founder of several sects, churches or religions.

If Jesus established his church, we must be able to find it.

Who is part of the Church of Christ?

Again, where is the true church? What has become of it? What are the signs for us that we can identify it? If we follow the biblical data, the appropriate belief wants us to accept that the Christian church is based on Jesus Christ, according to the revelation made to Peter in MATTHEW 16:16-18. He also stated that *"where two or three believers are gathered together in My name, I am there among them."* MATTHEW 18:20. The realization of this revelation took place at Pentecost. Under the influence of the Holy Spirit, many souls accepted the truth of Christ to be saved. Since then, whether in Jerusalem, Judea, Samaria, Caesarea, Cyprus, or Antioch, etc., the gospel is preached. The church represents all the people who have withdrawn from the secular practices to be part of the 'body of Christ'. (EPHESIANS 1:22,23). In a broader sense, it is referred to in many other things, including assembly, house of God, the Lord's vineyard, temple, woman, and the wife of the lamb. We also talk about local churches of various regions as part of the universal church. The spouse, of the Immaculate Lord, must be spotless to receive her husband who is Jesus Christ. Contrary to what all the tenets of different denominations are saying, the universal church transcends the chicanery and pettiness of the small chapels that spring up here and there. It is rather the assembly of believers united in Jesus Christ, the author and finisher of the faith of all Christians. The truth cannot be divided. It entails not only sincerity and humility, but due diligence to seek and find it, and the courage to implement it, at the expense of one's comfort zone. It causes changes that are often difficult to apply. It costs!

Apart from this tendency to take over the monopoly of salvation, some also are trumpeting that we live the post church era. The days of the church's existence are over. This message is increasingly echoed over time. It is wise to remember that God is omniscient. He knows and sees the end from the beginning. He declared that the gates of hell shall not prevail against his church. In John 10:15, 16, he not only gave his life for his sheep, but he will have more of them to come on board for everlasting life. The time will come for the Master to have one shepherd and one flock. In John 14:16-18, he promises not to leave the church orphaned, but to send a Comforter to be with it forever. According to Matthew 28:18-20, the church has a global mission to reach near and far, and preach the beloved Gospel to save lost souls. Jesus promised to remain committed and involved in his church's ministries until the end of the world. In I Corinthians 1:8,10, the apostle Paul said that the church must be blameless on the day of our Lord Jesus Christ. Acts 2:47 states that, "... *the Lord added to the church those who were saved.*" In other words, as soon as you receive the truth to be saved, the Lord leads you directly to the assembly of the redeemed.

If we stay in the spirit of Jesus, he seemed to focus on the imminent establishment of the Eternal Kingdom. He inaugurated his ministry by saying that the Kingdom of God is near (Mark 1:15). He wanted the gathering of all the followers, all those who through faith accept to belong to the new world order, the new system that he himself promotes and defends. The church becomes his means to gather the faithful, teach them the truth, and exhort them to be ready for the upcoming Advent. Alas, how often have we not made an end in itself? Instead of attracting people to Christ, we draw them to us, our religion, building, cathedral, pastor, and bishop. Instead of promoting the gospel, we preach bigotry. Instead of making the church a living organism, we make it a static organization.

- The church is not Christ, but it leads to Christ.
- The church is not the Kingdom of God, but it must lead believers into the Kingdom.
- The church is not the light, but it makes sense reflecting the divine light.
- The church is not the Gospel, but it must preach the Gospel of Jesus Christ.

Because of the reprehensible behavior of many believers, if a non-believer is interested in knowing anything about the Christian life, he or she may be confused by ideological disputes and dissenting voices heard everywhere. Too many currents of ideas, too many conflicts, too many negative/destructive competitions!

That's why millions of people are looking for unique values. They try different religions, ideas and theories borrowed from psychologists, sociologists, philosophers and modern theologians. Some even bring diverse ideas and practices from here and there to create their own credo which leads to a kind of religious syncretism. They miss the essence of authentic Christianity.

Authentic Christianity is not for sale. It is not a collection of laws, precepts. It is not necessarily a list of doctrines and beliefs, but a lifestyle practice and an active reflection of Jesus Christ. Many feel a great pleasure in talking about their religion, but true Christianity is about Christ and Christ alone. It is an active way to behave. It is revealed in the believer's way of life, his actions, conduct and relationship with the Supreme Being and his neighbor.

It is a relationship issue, but some like to make it a purely doctrinal, dogmatic case. We need more than a theoretical faith adorned with empty rituals. We need to show our belief in our way of life. The reality of the imminent establishment of the Kingdom of God should be guiding our lives and motivating our actions. One must always see Jesus in us in all aspects and circumstances of our lives. That is the constant challenge for every believer who, by the way, is an open book, and for many, the only open book in which the saving truth can be read.

When I was a child, I enjoyed reading everything I could lay my eyes and hands on. Needless to say that I sometimes read books that exceeded my level of understanding. The Bible is one of the books I devoured quickly without the ability to really grasp what it permeates. It took me several visits to this inexhaustible source to discover the pearls therein. I had to grow up, become more mature, and take time to meditate, develop a relationship with the real author of the Bible, and get His Spirit to penetrate in me so that I could more or less comprehend certain passages. It is a progressive way of life.

We are all influenced by the environment in which we operate. We are influenced by where we are born, who our parents are, the playgrounds, our educators, culture, financial conditions, values and even our color. We live in a century where things go very fast. This is a permissive society where almost everything is acceptable. This is the era of individualism. Unfortunately, the church is not immune to what is happening outside of it. It also seems to adopt this same individualistic, liberal philosophy that focuses on individuals choice and what they accept as a way of life. There is nothing absolute anymore. Everyone does as he or she pleases. The spiritual realm is not immune against this wave. The community spirit vanishes. It is replaced by all that is personal — my church, my pastor, my religion, my Jesus, my salvation, my faith, my doctrine, my life, my resurrection. Christianity has become a liberal caricature where every man takes the initiative to determine what is acceptable or not acceptable to him. God is put in a box that becomes smaller day after day.

Beloved, let us not delude ourselves. God condones the idea of community development and community assemblies; that is to say, a church where everything is done for the common good, where the condition of each member is taken into consideration with fairness and mercy while we are under God's leadership and waiting for His glorious return. This requires perseverance, courage, discipline and an indisputable dynamic Christianity. The ideal Christian community does not sell its faith and hope for the influence, popularity, and whatever this earthly life can offer us at the expense of the Eternal Kingdom. The ideal community seeks progress that is based on fairness, justice, respect and dignity for every being. It wants progress for the poor, to relieve the misery of the needy, and is interested in the welfare of every citizen.

A state of crisis within today's church.

Progress can be ambivalent. The tenors of progress may want to swim against the tide to serve their own advantages. When man speaks of success, make sure that he does not focus solely on a few people, or his small clique at the expense of the majority.

As part of continuous earthly crises, people are always complaining about the measurements of justice and the appropriate development and services for one group versus another. Real and unbiased provision for the welfare of every citizen to his satisfaction is an impossible challenge for all. The claims are multiplying. There is always a group that benefits and another group that suffers and is unhappy. Those who are frustrated, are looking for their opportunity to launch their claim and quest for justice. This is an ongoing struggle.

We read in the book of MATTHEW 20:25-28, *"Jesus called them unto him, and said, Ye know that the princes of the Gentiles exercise dominion over them, and they that are great exercise authority upon them. But it shall not be so among you: but whosoever will be great among you, let him be your minister; And whosoever will be chief among you, let him be your servant: Even as the Son of man came not to be ministered unto, but to minister, and to give his life a ransom for many."* It has been more than 20 centuries since humanity heard these words of the Savior who left the earth with the promise of returning for his church. What kind of church will he return here to take? The ecclesial community must have a different philosophy and approach.

Jesus does not give us the name of a particular church or the date, but we have distinctive signs to identify it and to know that we are approaching that special time.

What are the distinctive signs to identify the Church of Christ?

1. According to 1 Timothy 3:15, it is defined as the house of the living God, the pillar and ground of the truth.

2. It is a dynamic assembly that receives divine approval.

To ease the task and engage in sensible endeavor, why not revisit the times of early Christianity to find the model that can guide us to support our beliefs? Indeed, the Acts of the Apostles, more specifically, chapter 2, verses 42-47 tell us that, "*They devoted themselves to the apostles' teaching, the fellowship, the breaking of bread and prayers. The fear came upon every soul, and he did many wonders and miracles through the apostles. All who believed were together, and they had everything in common. They sold their possessions and goods, and they shared the proceeds among all, according to individual needs. They were together every day frequent the temple, and breaking bread in their homes and shared their food with gladness and singleness of heart, praising God and having favor with all the people. And the Lord added to the church daily those who were saved.*"

The book of Acts of the Apostles tells the story of the origins of Christianity, a church crystallized under the control of the Holy Spirit who was able to manifest Himself through the use of languages, or miracles. The Holy Spirit controlled and administered the ways and means to spread the Gospel.

Simple criteria to choose a Christian church:

1. It must be based on Jesus Christ, the rock of all ages in words and actions

2. The Bible must be the source of its teaching, its doctrine and its principles, no picking and choosing. This includes the entire Bible.

3. Biblical teachings must take precedence over the traditions and culture.

4. Conduct of officers should be based on Jesus's life of prayer and concern for the welfare of the flock of God

5. The goal of the church is simple: to save souls for Christ through the preaching of the gospel and taking care of the needs of all who attend.

Ten Characteristics of The True Church

How do we define the role of the church? As a dynamic assembly, it is there to exhort, instruct, encourage and strengthen the faith of those who take the path that leads to everlasting life in Christ, while ensuring their development to their full potential during their passage on earth. The original church is the prototype that deserves our attention. The core text for this chapter is found in the Acts of the Apostles, including chapter 2, verses 42-47.

I. The Basis Of The Authentic Church

"Jesus Christ himself being the chief cornerstone."
Ephesians 2:20

It remains an undeniable fact that the success, duration and extent of a building depends on its ability to withstand the rigors of its environment and to pass squarely the required tests for its existence. It all depends on its foundation. The success of skyscrapers in withstanding any challenge of nature, and even criminal acts, is base on their foundation. If the architect, engineer, builder or owner is careless, frugal and lazy, he will have one of the most unpleasant surprises of a lifetime. If the materials that were used to erect the building were defective, of poor or insufficient quality, the building will collapse and bring shame and even criminal charges against its builders. Therefore, the need for rigor and accuracy become unparalleled, especially when we must lay the foundation of a spiritual building.

Needless to say, it is crucial that the true church has a strong foundation. In light of the Bible, there is no better basis for the Assembly of Saints but Jesus Christ. He is the Solid Rock; the corner stone that cannot be abandoned by anyone who wants a firm foundation for the church. We cannot dare to speak of the ideal church, without knowing Jesus Christ, his instructions, his life, his goal, and his requirements. The church does not exist outside its sole founder. Jesus is the head who makes it the living organism. Christ and the church are inseparable.

Jesus Christ: The foundation of the Church.

How do we know that Jesus Christ is the foundation of his church? What are the signs of an assembly in which Jesus Christ is the cornerstone?

Why Jesus Christ and nobody else?

To answer this question properly, it is worth beginning by asking Who Jesus Christ is. The prophet Isaiah, who lived during the second half of the 8th century B.C. predicted the coming of the Messiah in Isaiah 7:14. *"Therefore the Lord himself will give you a sign, behold, a virgin shall conceive, and bear a son, and shall call his name Immanuel."* In Isaiah 9:6 he says of the Messiah, *"For unto us a child is born, unto us a son is given: and the government shall be upon his shoulder: and his name shall be called wonderful, Counselor, the Mighty God, the everlasting Father, the Prince of Peace."* In The Gospel of St. Matthew, in the first chapter, according verses 18-21, Mary was pregnant, by the power of the Holy Spirit, and would have a son named Jesus who will save his people from their sins. In Revelations 3:7, He describes Himself as "... *the Saint, the truth, who has the key of David, who opens and no one closes, who closes and no one shall open.*" Jesus said in JOHN 14:6, "*I am the way, truth and life.*" Or in JOHN 8:58, "*Jesus said unto them, 'Verily, verily I say unto you, Before Abraham was, I am'.*" Contrary to what some philosophers say, Jesus did not become the son of God after having led a Holy life.

These verses identify and affirm his pre-existence. **John 1:1** says, "*In the beginning was the Word, the Word was with God and the Word was God.*" According to EPHESIANS 1:22, it is God himself who gave the Lord Jesus Christ to the Supreme Head of the Church. In EPHESIANS 5:23, 25 and 29, the apostle Paul wrote that Christ is the head of the church, which is his body, and he is the Savior. Christ loves the church and gave himself for it ... Christ nourishes the church. During his pilgrimage on this earth, Jesus declared in JOHN 15:5, "*I am the vine, ye are the branches: He that abides in me, and I in him, the same brings forth much fruit: for without me ye can do nothing.*"

In the book of ACTS of the Apostles, written by Luke, a Physician, chapter 4 verse 12 we read, "*Neither is there salvation in any other: for there is under heaven no other name given among men, whereby we must be saved.*"

In light of these texts and many others, we can conclude that a church that wants to continue to function according to God's will and that intends to keep growing under the watchful eyes of the Almighty, cannot have any other foundation but that of Jesus Christ. When Christ said to Peter in MATTHEW 16:18 "*Thou art Peter (Cephas) and on this rock I will build my church.*" This should not be misunderstood as according a hierarchy over the church to Saint Peter. Of course, Peter was a zealous apostle who did great things in his ecclesial ministry, but he is not the basis of the church. Indeed, shortly after hearing these sublime words of the Lord in verse 23 of the same chapter, the Master had to rebuke Peter saying *"Get thee behind me, Satan!"* The fact remains, the true church is founded on Jesus Christ, the author and finisher of our faith and who is flawless at all time. He alone died for us. He alone gives us salvation. In JOHN 14:6 we read, *"No one comes to the Father except through Me."* Beyond any shadow of doubt, the authentic church is built upon the Rock of all ages, Jesus!

As such, the church should follow his orders and must follow his example in everything. *"He that saith he abideth in him ought himself also so to walk, even as he walked"*, 1 JOHN 2:6. What was the life of Jesus? *"My meat is to do the will of him that sent me, and to finish his work."* JOHN 4:34

In conclusion: Is Jesus the foundation of your church?

How do we know that a church has Jesus Christ at its base and at its head? When it cares enough to ensure that salvation is free and accessible to all without distinction. The true church leads its members to Christ to have eternal life. Being saved by grace, it strives to put into practice everything that is in God's book without any exception. It chooses to stand for the truth rather than to enjoy or benefit from the practices of the secular world. It is a worthy representative of the gospel that must not only speak of Christ and defend his doctrine, but also reflect Christ daily by responding to community needs. According to MATTHEW 9:35, Jesus preached, taught and healed. He cared for the spiritual, physical and material needs of his contemporaries. What are the signs of an assembly which has Jesus Christ as its cornerstone? It follows in the footsteps of Jesus' ministry without turning to the right or to the left. Jesus gave a clear summary of his mission in Luke 4:20-25, John 14:6, and John 8:12. To agree to follow him requires a radical change. The following texts: Matthew 5:48, 7:21, 10:32, 16:24-26, John 13:34, John 15:12-17, and Matthew 28:19-20 give us a road map of what is expected from an authentic Christian assembly and from every believer who operates under God's leadership and has His approval.

Throughout the gospels, we can see the essential of Jesus Christ's ministry: He was always compassionate, he went everywhere, teaching in the synagogues, preaching the gospel of the kingdom, healing every disease and sickness of the people, while the defenders of the established system, watched, hated him and tried to kill him. Why? A major reason for the constant opposition between Jesus on one side, the scribes, the Pharisees and religious leaders, on the other side, turned around the true worship, the real truth. The Jews gave priority to appearance. 1 Samuel 16:7 tells us: "*The man looks to those who beat me, but the Lord looketh on the heart.*" Jewish leaders in power could not stand him because of prejudice. They were hypocritical legalists who engaged in trying to discover new ways to make the observance of divine laws stricter and more cumbersome. Jesus was just the opposite "*my yoke is easy and my burden is light*" Matthew 11:30. They lacked the essential for the true servants of God, love, mercy, humility, compassion, and zeal to serve the population. Jesus said in Matthew 20:26 "*Whoever wants to be first among you must be your slave."* If we read MATTHEW 9:9-17, 32-34, MATTHEW 11:19-24 or MATTHEW 12:53-58 or MATTHEW 15:2-9, MATTHEW 16:1-2 and 19:3, or MATTHEW 21:15, 16, 23, 45, 41, or MATTHEW 22:15-46, MATTHEW 23, or MATTHEW 26:3, 4; 27:1 or MARK, LUKE or JOHN, we discover a common fact: the priests, the scribes and the elders were all opposed to Jesus, because His understanding of the sacred ministry was to teach, preach, feed the hungry, heal the sick and doing good wherever he went.

II. The Authentic Light of a Genuine Church

"Your word is a lamp to my feet, and a light unto my path."
PSALMS 119:105

It is obvious that light plays a pivotal role in the daily activities of life. Until my teenage years, I spent my life in a city where the rupture of the electricity was religiously performed at any time of day and night. You can imagine the impact of such a situation on the population in almost all areas of life. Students had to accommodate themselves or their future was at the mercy of the electric company. Sometimes the street lights also were out. It affected the studies of several kids who were going to bed late while the parents stood guard to wake them up if the electric current came back on. I still remember those devilish moments.

They were not pleasant. Businesses had to find a way around that challenge. The fact remains that we cannot do much in darkness. We are afraid that we may face certain harmful or even fatal objects. We may do harm to ourselves or others if we venture into the dark without knowing where we are heading. Dangers may await us and threaten us. Lighting is manifested by degrees. It is rare to find someone who would have preferred a small kerosene lamp instead of a complete lighting and sophisticated system once he has access to the modern way of doing things. If physical or mental darkness can cost us dearly, spiritual darkness is even more devastating because it affects not only our existence here on this earth, but it also affects our eternal destiny. If we seek to have the best lighting for our secular affairs, it is also important that we find the best lighting for our spiritual growth. **No light source compares to the sacred oracles.** They are a treasure that deserves our attention. *"You search the scriptures because you think you have eternal life in it: what are they which testify of me,"* (JOHN 5:39). The sacred oracles represent a unique way to know the whole truth and to walk in the light that leads to eternal life. This is why we appreciate the cry of our predecessors, *Sola Scriptura*. We live in an era of sophisticated people who question everything. The authority and authenticity of the Bible are challenged by many. People want to find what justifies their philosophies, beliefs and behavior. They use their own interpretation and find texts here and there just to twist them and make them support their philosophy, to exonerate themselves of their unbelief and clear themselves of their guilt. Some go so far as to classify the Bible as one book among others and give it no special importance or preference. Another category of people said that the Bible is 'a book' among other important spiritual books of life. Beloved, **the Bible is the only source of light for the obedient believer.** JAMES 1:22 tells us to be 'doers' of the word and not to tie ourselves to human reasoning that is deceitful.

The church depends entirely on the Bible. It recognizes it as the word of God to the human race. The true church of God is engaged in teaching and following biblical doctrine. Its passion is to constantly explore the scriptures and to put into practice what the Bible teaches without turning to the right or to the left. It is worthwhile to imitate the example of early Christians. We must develop a natural love for learning and constantly feed ourselves from the words of the Master. The Christian should live a theological life by developing a constant passion to study about God and ask Him for guidance in his daily life.

ACTS 2:42 says, "*They continued steadfastly in the teaching Apostles.*" ACTS 17:2 says, "*Paul went in as usual. For three Sabbaths reasoned with them from the Scriptures.*" In verse 11, "*These Jews were more noble than those in Thessalonica, in that they received the message with great eagerness and examined the Scriptures daily to see if what Paul said was true.*"

ACTS 18:28 says, "*For he powerfully refuted the Jews publicly, showing by the Scriptures that Jesus is the Christ.*" 2 TIMOTHY 3:16, 17 says, "*All Scripture is God-breathed and profitable for teaching, for reproof, for correction, for instruction in righteousness: That the man of God may be thoroughly equipped for every good work.*" PSALMS 119:11 says, "***Thy word have I hid in mine heart, that I might not sin against thee.***"

III. Prayer — The Source of Oxygen For The Church

"***Pray God that he will be gracious unto us.***"
MALACHI 1:9

Imagine a building with everything you can ever dream of, the most extravagant and most expensive furniture in an upscale neighborhood where everything is beautiful and exquisite. When the day of its inauguration comes, all of society's dignitaries are there for such an event. Everything was planned, but they forgot one key thing. They did not make provisions for air conditioning. With a temperature above 100 degrees or below 0 degrees Fahrenheit, how many would believe that such a launch would be a success? Certainly no one would think it is normal to construct a building without planning a reliable cooling/heating system that can withstand any condition. Otherwise, the building could not undergo the rigors of the seasons. It would not receive its certificate of occupancy. The occupants would abandon such a place. It might be vandalized and eventually collapse. If an adequate heating/cooling system is not optional for a building, especially in countries where the seasons change from one extreme to another, needless to say that God's church cannot exist without **prayer**. We read in Acts 2:42 that, *"They devoted themselves to prayers."* That is to say, their lives revolved around prayer. In 1 Timothy 2:1, the apostle Paul declares, ***"I exhort therefore, that, first of all, supplications, prayers, intercessions, and giving of thanks, be made for all men."*** He continues in verse 8 of the same chapter, ***"Will therefore that men pray every where, lifting up holy hands, without wrath and doubting."***

The psalmist writes in Psalm 65:2, *"O you who hear prayer! All men will come"*. The wise man said in Proverbs 15:8, 29 that the prayer of the upright is pleasing to the Lord. He hears the prayer of the righteous. In Isaiah 56:7, the prophet recalls the divine desire that *"My house shall be called a house of prayer for all peoples."*

Luke reminds us in Acts 1:14 that all of one accord continued steadfastly in prayer. Paul, in Ephesians 6:18 said, ***"Praying always with all prayer and supplication in the Spirit, and watching thereunto with all perseverance and supplication for all saints."*** There is no doubt that the ideal Christian Assembly must always pray. Besides, while on this earth, Jesus himself spent hours, nights and days in prayer to claim power from his Father above to fulfill his mission. If you belong to an assembly where prayers are lacking or are not a priority, you must use tact and gentleness to urge its leaders to get back on their knees and pray. In reality, the church has no higher calling but to live a prayerful life, not only in order to seek the permanent presence of the Very High in its midst but also to claim divine favors for the faithful and protection against the arrows of the enemy. Matthew 26:41 *"Watch and Pray."*

IV. A Dynamic Assembly That Serves Its Community

"If thou canst do anything, have compassion on us, and help us." **Mark 9:22.**

According to Matthew 20, starting with verse 20, Jesus answered the request of the sons of Zebedee by saying that "whoever wants to become great among you, let him be your servant." This statement served as a backdrop for the ministry of our Lord. During his short stay on earth, he never missed an opportunity to show his passion for souls. For example, we can cite the multiplication of fish and loaves (Matthew 14:13-21 and MATTHEW 15:23-39). The early church is described as, *"They devoted themselves to fraternal communion, the breaking of bread. All who believed were together, and they had everything in common. They sold their possessions and goods, and parted the product of all, according to individual needs."* (ACTS 2:42-46). MATTHEW 14:16 says, *"Jesus answered them: they do not need to go away, give them something to eat."*

JAMES 2:15, 16 says, *"If a brother or sister be naked, and destitute of daily food, and one of you say unto them: depart in peace, be ye warmed and filled; notwithstanding ye give them not those things which are needful to the body; what doth it profit?"*

"Pure religion and undefiled before God and the Father is this, To visit the fatherless and widows in their affliction, and to keep himself unspotted from the world." (JAMES 1:27).

MATTHEW 9:35, 36 says, *"Jesus went about all the cities and villages, teaching in their synagogues, preaching the gospel of the kingdom, and healing every disease and every infirmity. Seeing the crowds, he had compassion for her, because they were troubled and abandoned, like sheep without a shepherd."*

Jude 3 says, "Beloved, I was very eager to write you about our common salvation."

3 JOHN 2 says, ***"Beloved, I wish above all things that thou mayest prosper and be in health, even as thy soul prospereth."*** The gauge to measure an assembly's commitment to serving the Lord is its dedication to serving the community. Note that the early church had a comprehensive approach. Everything was shared and

voluntary. The church was rushing to the rescue of all those in need. This is mentioned by the apostle in 1 Corinthians 12:4-31. We are all members of one body under the leadership of the Holy Spirit. Each of us can understand easily that the human body is made up of many parts, yet they are all connected and united. The heart cannot take all the blood and self appropriate it exclusively. The lungs cannot keep all the oxygen to themselves. If one part of the body decided to 'boycott' another part or to ignore or mistreat the rest of the body, ultimately, it would end up destroying the entire body. It is an interdependent relationship. The trials and tribulations or the challenges of any member of that body should concern us all. The ideal functioning of the body of Christ is the way the human body functions. 'Koinonia' is a very important Greek word in the life of the early church. It represents a community whose mentality and spirit are molded with the desire to gather everything together for a fair share according to the needs of the community.

V. An Organized Assembly That Condones Hierarchical Order and Respect of Principles

"I see with joy your order, and the steadfastness of your faith in Christ." Colossians 2:5

Whatever the location, purpose or type of organization, a company cannot endure or thrive in anarchy. The history of civilization shows that the time of decline is at hand when citizens are no longer organized in a coherent fashion. There is no respect for authority. Everyone is pursuing his small selfish ends to the detriment of the common good and refuses to recognize a single authority. Shared values are put on hold. Justice, stability, security, and respect give way to abuses, vices, corruption, dictatorship, torture, and passion for pleasure. It is the reign of degradation, lack of cohesion, lack of collaboration, disobedience leading toward the general stampede and the collapse of the system.

We read in MATTHEW 12:25 that a house divided will be destroyed. In the primitive church, people *"continued steadfastly in the apostles' teaching."* (ACTS 2:42). People were still willing to listen, learn and be taught. 1 CORINTHIANS 14:40 says, *"Let all things be done with decency and order."* ACTS 13:1, 2 says *"There was in the church doctors, prophets, …"* The apostle Paul mentions the different talents and different roles of members 'for the edification of the whole assembly'. The major concern is to contribute to peace and mutual edification. ROMANS 14:19 says, ***"Let us therefore follow after the things which make for peace, and things wherewith one may edify another."***

HEBREWS 13:17 tells us, *"Obey your leaders and to have the greatest respect for them because they watch over your souls as to render account; they pose is so, so they've done so with joy, and not with grief, what would you do any benefit."* In other words, in the House of the Lord, everyone has a role and a ministry that cares about enough to do it with their best ability. The church prays, fasts and acts under the influence of the Holy Spirit who guides it every step of the way. Everyone has a place and is properly valued. No one's work is despised or neglected . The leaders appreciate it and gave testimony. The leaders also are appreciated and respected.

REVELATIONS 2:5 says, *"Remember therefore from whence thou art fallen, repent you, and do the first works, or*

I will come unto thee, and will remove thy candlestick out of its place, unless thou repent." The remnant church must ensure that all its members are active.

EPHESIANS 4:11-15 presents the diversity of gifts in the unity of the faith. This is not a false promise of absolute equality, but the exercise of love, fairness and respect for all to work together to achieve the objectives of the body and the distribution of services according to everyone's needs and possibilities. Not to neglect the support provided in time of trials and tribulations. ROMANS 13:2 says, *"Do not resist authority."* The interpretation also includes the role of the authority of the church who works under Jesus Christ, the ultimate authority.

VI.-a An Assembly Guided By The Holy Spirit

"Behold, I will pour out my spirit unto you."
PROVERBS 1:23

What sumptuous building equipped with everything under the sun would be occupied if the builder had neglected to put a roof on it? It would have been a definite sign of madness, wouldn't you say? In the church, the Holy Spirit covers us all and protects us from the vicious storms of life. He plays various roles and is very active in God's Assembly.

"The Lord added daily to the church those who were saved," (ACTS 2:47B).

ZECHARIAH 4:6 says, *"Thus says the Lord, this is neither by force nor by power but by my Spirit."*

EPHESIANS 5:18 says, ***"And be not drunk with wine, wherein is excess; but be filled with the Spirit."***

JOEL 2:28 says, *"I will pour my spirit upon all flesh."*

The church can have everything it needs in the eyes of this world, but if it does not have the Holy Spirit of God, it will remain stagnant, divided, frustrated, selfish, lukewarm, careless and even corrupt. A church without the Holy Spirit has missed the mark. It walks in darkness, it has lost its way, and it goes astray. The secular world appreciates the success and impact of an institution on a community by its assets, financial strength, scope of influence, social and economic standings, and presence in the Day-to-day mundane events. What matters to God is an assembly of faithful servants who act under the impetus of his Holy Spirit. So many times in our society, our assemblies are filled with something that pushes them to engage in all types of activities. But no one can know for sure if it is the Holy Spirit. The authentic church must be sure it operates under the sole guidance of the Holy Spirit.

VI.-b An Assembly That Has The Fruit of The Spirit

"Bring forth therefore fruits meet for repentance."
MATTHEW 3:8

GALATIANS 5:22 *"But the fruit of the Spirit is love, joy, peace, patience, kindness, goodness, faithfulness, gentleness, temperance."*

EPHESIANS 5:9 says *"The fruit of light consists in all goodness, justice and truth."*

The members of the early church were usually together; they ate together with gladness and simplicity and enjoyed the fruit of the spirit. How do we know? They loved each other and were happy sharing their daily bread. They practice patience, kindness, goodness, faithfulness and gentleness toward each other.

PROVERBS 29:23 says, *"A man's pride shall bring him low: but honour shall uphold the humble in spirit."*

1 PETER 3:8 says *"Finally, be ye all of one mind, having compassion one of another, love as brethren, be pitiful, and be courteous."*

COLOSSIANS 2:18 says, *"Let no man beguile you of your reward in a voluntary humility and worshipping of angels, intruding into those things which he hath not seen, vainly puffed up by his fleshly mind."*

EPHESIANS 4:1,2 says, *"I therefore, the prisoner of the Lord, beseech you that ye walk worthy of the vocation wherewith ye are called, With all lowliness and meekness, with long-suffering, forbearing one another in love."*

Allow this peculiarity: A church where the Spirit of God reigns is joyful. That may seem paradoxical to many, but it is biblical. According to ISAIAH 9:2, God provides joy.

PSALM 100:1 says *"Make a joyful noise unto the LORD, all ye lands."*

COLOSSIANS 1:11 says that through God's glorious power we can have happiness, endurance and patience.

1 THESSALONIANS 5:16 says, *"Rejoice evermore."*

PROVERBS 15:15 says *"He that is of a merry heart hath a continual feast."*

PROVERBS 17:22 ***"A merry heart doeth good like a medicine: but a broken spirit drieth the bones."***

May we think about our relationship with God and with our fellows. May we be a source of comfort and joy for our brothers and sisters in Christ and for the world.

VII. An Assembly That Praises God And Worships His Name

"All the earth shall worship thee, and shall sing unto thee."
PSALMS 66:4

"They praised God and found favor with all the people." Praising means applaud to applaud or appreciate someone. For many reasons, sometimes we feel obligated to praise people in a key position, although we resent it. This is not the case for God. He is worthy to be praised all the time.

2 CHRONICLES 5:11-14 says, ***"When the priests were come out of the holy place, (for all the priests that were present were sanctified, and did not then wait by course:*** *Also the Levites which were the singers, all of them of Asaph, of Heman, of Jeduthun, with their sons and their brethren, being arrayed in white linen, having cymbals and psalteries and harps, stood at the east end of the altar, and with them an hundred and twenty priests sounding with trumpets:) It came even to pass, as the trumpeters and singers were as one, to make one sound to be heard in praising and thanking the LORD; and when they lifted up their voice with the trumpets and cymbals and instruments of musick, and praised the LORD, saying, For he is good; for his mercy endureth for ever: that then the house was filled with a cloud, even the house of the LORD;So that the priests could not stand to*

minister by reason of the cloud: for the glory of the LORD had filled the house of God."

EPHESIANS 5:19 says, ***"Speaking to yourselves in psalms and hymns and spiritual songs, singing and making melody in your heart to the Lord."***

Unfortunately, there are many churches that contain people who are just going through the motions, like robots. They perform by automatism but their hearts are far from it. These people are dull, indifferent, and empty, with no energy. They reflect disdain, discouragement, and depression. Through the way they offer a service to their God, such members give no reason for a visitor to return. The churches that please God sing full of life, with delight and celebrate and praise the Lord who has done great things for them. A church that does not praise is either ungrateful or resents God for not doing enough for its institution or members. This may sound controversial, but let us be clear. We are not talking about putting on a show or making a lot of noise and having people's emotions run high. No! We are talking about genuine sense of thanksgiving, gratitude toward the Lord of Lords for what he has done for us. We praise him for what he does and we worship him for who He is. The authentic church praises God for who he is and brings forth thanksgivings for being alive. It gives shouts of praises and encourages all who attend.

The church is joyful and praises and recognizes the goodness of the Lord. The visitor then leaves such a meeting encouraged with joy, a warm heart, a feeling of having been welcomed, loved and energized. This stimulates a desire to return.

VIII. An Evangelical Assembly

"God trust us with the gospel." 1 Thessalonians 2:4

The church has a genuine mission to preach and prepare souls for Christ. It draws the saved. Matthew 9:37 says, *"Then Jesus told his disciples, the harvest is plentiful but the workers are few."* Matthew 28:19-20 says *"Go, teach all nations, baptizing them in the name of the Father, Son and Holy Spirit, teaching them to obey everything I have commanded you. And surely I am with you always, until the end of the world." "The church had peace throughout Judea, Galilee, Samaria, edified and walking in the fear of the Lord, and it grew by the help of the Holy Spirit."* (Acts 9:31). The church is not an exclusive club where privileged members gather to relax and enjoy the benefits of their contributions. It is rather a meeting led by the Holy Spirit who takes the initiative to cement the faith of believers and leads them in a place where they can grow in all aspects of their existence. The Spirit illuminates the minds and opens the hearts that are sincere enough to receive the message that saves. However, the church must be truly willing to proclaim the good news not just in words but in actions. When a meeting is evolving with zeal, love, unity, peace, and concern about the welfare of its members, those who observe it can see the difference to the point of wanting to know more about it.

IX. An Assembly Where The Leaders Perform Miracles

"The signs of an apostle were wrought among you with mighty deeds." 2 Corinthians 12:12

A church where the leaders are filled with the Holy Spirit can meet the needs of its community. There are instances when miracles need to be performed, not to show off, but because of its necessity to strengthen the faith of the believers. In ACTS 2:43, we read that the Apostles were able to do many miracles for the population. According to MATTHEW 7:22 and MATTHEW 24:24, being able to perform miracles is not a guarantee that God approves of you as His distinguished servant, but those who are really connected to God, when they pray earnestly, usually get a positive result.

MATTHEW 10:1 says, *"Having called his 12 disciples, he gave them power to expel evil spirits and to heal every disease and infirmity."*

MATTHEW 17:19-21 says, *"...the disciples came to Jesus, and he said in particular: why do we not have cast him? Because of your unbelief, said Jesus. I tell you the truth, if you have faith as a mustard seed, ye shall say to this mountain, carrying up by then, and it shall remove; nothing will be impossible. But this kind goeth not out but by prayer and fasting."*

MARK 16:17,18 says, *"And these signs will accompany those who believe: In my name they will cast out demons, they speak with new tongues, they shall take up serpents and if they drink any deadly thing, it will do them no harm they will lay hands on the sick, and sick be cured."* These words of Jesus should not be taken out of context. The miracle of the servants of God is performed with humility and without pomp or wanting to be deified in place of the King of Kings. It does not lead to going out looking for mortal beverages to drink. It says, *"If they drink anything deadly, it will do them no harm."* If while working in God's ministry you happen to be set up, or someone decides to poison you, certainly the Lord will intervene, but this should not be a practice to go to seek out such circumstances and assume that God will intervene. This would be presumptuous. God does not condone such behavior. The Christian is meek and humble of heart, as his Master, when he was on earth. The Bible relates various examples of the miraculous intervention of Jesus. In Acts 14:18-20, Paul healed a cripple. Acts 5:12-16, Acts 8:7 and Acts 28:9 provide other examples.

James 5:14-16 says, *"Is anyone among you sick? That call for the elders of the church, and let them pray over him, anointing him with oil in the name of the Lord's prayer of faith shall save the sick and the Lord shall raise him and if he has committed sins, he will be pardoned. Confess your sins to each other and pray for one another, that ye may be healed. The prayer of a righteous man is powerful and effective."* The church leaders must implore the Lord in humility for the Shepherd to honor their ministry by giving them the privilege to pray for the faithful and see the results, not to boast, but to continue to praise Jehovah.

X. An Assembly Sorely Tried, Then Rewarded

"After being tried, one shall receive the crown of life."
James 1:12

Since the Lord's church does not participate in the mundane things on this earth, but instead invites the world to turn from its wicked ways, the church will be detested, persecuted, humiliated and attempts will be made to annihilate it. While we appreciate the success of the early church, if we want to have a congregation of the same kind, we cannot overlook the fact that it was persecuted. When early Christians agreed to come under the banner of Prince Emmanuel, they received very little encouragement from established institutions, or the majority of people in their time. Instead, they were mocked, persecuted and martyred. However, God never abandoned them. Several had to seal their alliance in the Christian faith by their blood. Yet they felt privileged to be able to share in the suffering of the Master.

2 Timothy 3:12 says, *"All who live godly in Christ Jesus will be persecuted."*

John 15:20 says, *"If they persecuted me, they will persecute you too."*

Matthew 5:10-12 says, *"Blessed are those who are persecuted for righteousness, for so persecuted they the prophets which were before you."*

Matthew 10:38 says, *"Whoever does not take his cross and follow me is not worthy of me."*

Matthew 16:24 says, *"Then Jesus told his disciples: If anyone would come after me, let him deny himself, let him take up his cross and follow me."*

Mark 10:28-30 says, *"Then Peter began to say: here we have left all and followed thee. Jesus answered, I tell you the truth, there is no one who has left because of me and because of the good news, his house, or brothers or sisters or mother or father, or children, or lands, shall receive a hundredfold now in this century, houses, brothers, sisters, mothers, children, and lands, with persecutions, and in the world to come eternal life."*

REVELATIONS 7:9-17 says, *"After this I looked, and behold, there was a great multitude that no one could count, from every nation, every tribe, every people, and tongues. They stood before the throne and before the Lamb, clothed in white robes, and palms in their hands. And they cried with a loud voice, saying: salvation is our God who sits on the throne, and unto the Lamb. And all the angels stood around the throne and the elders and the four living creatures, and they fell on their faces before the throne and worshipped God, saying: Amen! Praise, glory, wisdom, and thanksgiving, honor, power and strength be to our God for ever and ever Amen And one of the elders answered, saying to me: those who are clothed in white robes, who are they and where did they come from? I said: My Lord, you know. And he said, they are those who came out of great tribulation and have washed their robes and made them white in the blood of the lamb.*

"They will be no longer hungry, they will no longer be thirsty, and the sun shall not strike them, nor any heat. For the Lamb which is in the midst of the throne will shepherd them and lead them to springs of living water, and God will wipe every tear from their eyes."

Do you recognize your church in the above characteristics?

Certainly the authentic church will never persecute people. Instead, it will be persecuted by others. It will never be popular and loved by the entire world for long. It needs to flee liberalism, rationalism, and the desire to be politically correct and popular.

The church of the Lord must prepare itself for the terrible days that will fall upon it. That is why Christians should take advantage of the time allotted to them to read, meditate, preach and get closer to the Lord of Lords and King of Kings. The church needs to preach the gospel to all around it and serve God in a sincere and decisive way. Soon it will no longer enjoy the privilege of meeting in its impressive and beautiful cathedral, but will instead have to hide in mountains, caves and cellars to escape the wrath of the enemies who, yesterday, were among their most trusted allies and family members. *"If those days were not shortened, no flesh would be saved."* (Matthew 24:22). We must follow Jesus alone, so when the hard times fall upon us, when the rebels of the earth have to face the days of serious crises, **when the abomination of desolation will be seen even in the holy place**, (Matthew 24:15) that is to say, when the 'so called' Christians will become the main sources of blasphemy and disgrace to the cause of Christ, the Remnant must be vigilant, persevering and careful. In 2 Timothy 3:1-9 we find a partial list of the situation at the end of time. Above all, the church of God will triumph and reign with God for eternity.

Summary.

The church led by God embodies respect, teaches and practices what its Master wants it to teach, and remains faithful to the fundamental principles of Christianity without wishing to add or subtract even a comma. It perseveres in fellowship, prayer, simplicity, humility and wisdom. It ensures the welfare of its individual members, it yearns and cares for the salvation of souls, and it praises the Lord. It is happy, well organized, and is constantly under the influence of the

Holy Spirit. It is united. Its consecrated leaders can do miracles and heal the sick. It is a church that succeeds with God and because it is successful, it becomes the enemy's target who swears to wage war against God's select even at heaven's gate. But JOHN 16:33 tells us "... *In the world ye shall have tribulation: but be of good cheer; I have overcome the world.*" (JOHN 16:33).

Here is our road map for the authentic church that you and I should join. In good conscience, can we say that we are part of the true church? Dear concerned readers, what shall we do?

REVELATIONS 3:19 says, *"Be zealous therefore and repent."* This is the Jesus's declaration to the church of Laodicea.

In Conclusion:

Beloved, we cannot delude ourselves. As life on this planet becomes increasingly difficult with all sorts of accidents, disasters, terrors, crimes, and misfortunes happening everywhere, Jesus Christ is at the door. It is time to take things seriously without deciding to set a date. Let's take inventory of ourselves. Let's do it now! If I have spoken evil or erred, show me where I misstepped through the biblical texts in a firm and unequivocal fashion.

Let us avoid navigating in a pool of innuendos and stretching the texts here and there to make them agree with us. It is not the Bible that has to agree with us. We are to be in harmony with what the Bible says. Remember, the devil used verses to tempt Jesus, the son of God, according to MATTHEW 4:1-10. If he had the audacity to quote the Bible out of its context in front of the author of that Bible, can you imagine what he can do to make us think and believe in things that are far from the truth? You and I must do something. It is what I call **the fundamental schema of Christianity,** summarized in 4 steps:

1. Encounter with the Lord God through various ways and means (media, books, personal contacts, etc).

2. Accept his call and salvation by grace and be overwhelmed by his love.

3. Acquire knowledge and share his words with others.

4. Grow in grace and obey his will until his return.

Ultimately, if you need one key sentence to characterize the church's remains, see REVELATIONS 14:12, *"Here is the patience of the saints: here are they that keep the commandments of God, and the faith of Jesus".* REVELATIONS 19:10 *"for the testimony of Jesus is the spirit of prophecy."*

The faith of Jesus is the spirit of prophecy. Joel tells us in JOEL 2:28, *"And it shall come to pass afterward, that I will pour out my spirit upon all flesh; and your sons and your daughters shall prophesy, your old men shall dream dreams, your young men shall see visions."*

If you want a brief description of the duty of the true church during the last days, read REVELATIONS 14:6-11 *"I saw another angel flying in mid heaven, having the everlasting gospel to preach to the inhabitants of the earth, at any nation, every tribe, and tongue, and every people. He said in a loud voice: Fear God and give him glory because the hour of His Judgment is come: and worship Him who made heaven and earth and sea and springs . And another, a second angel followed, saying, Babylon is fallen, is fallen, Babylon the great, who has made all nations drink the wine of the wrath of her fornication! And another, a third angel followed them, saying with a loud voice, If anyone worships the beast and his image and receives his mark on his forehead or his hand, he himself shall also drink the wine of God's wrath, poured unmixed into the cup of his wrath, and he will be tormented with fire and brimstone before the holy angels and before the Lamb. And the smoke of their torment ascends forever and ever: and they have no rest day nor night, who worship the beast and his image, and whoever receives the mark of his name."*

This is the moment to take a leap of faith. Take inventory of your relationship with the Almighty and ask Him to guide you and to help you make the right decision. The sooner, the better!

Where is the Church of the Lord? Where are we? Where are you in the race to eternal life? What are we doing for the Lord now?

MATTHEW 11:12 says, "*... **the kingdom of heaven suffereth violence, and the violent take it by force.***"

MATTHEW 24:45-51 says, "*What then is the faithful and prudent servant, that his master has set over his household, to give them meat in due season? Blessed is that servant whom his master on his arrival, find so doing! I tell you the truth, he set him over all his possessions. But if that evil servant shall say in himself: My lord delays to come, if he begins to beat his companions to eat and drink with drunkards, the master of that servant will come the day he does not expect At a time and it does not master, and put it in pieces, and appoint him his portion with the hypocrites: there shall be weeping and gnashing of teeth."*

The return of Jesus Christ must not be a surprise for his true church. Under the influence of the Holy Spirit, the authentic church is zealous for good deeds. It praises the name of the Creator, advocates love, peace, and success for of all of its members, and finally prays fervently for God to protect and lead it to the final port. Beloved, is this what your church looks like? If not, what role do you play to help achieve this? If you are looking for a true Assembly of God, this information should help you find the true church to strengthen your faith and help you maintain your relationship with God while helping your neighbor. Christianity advocates a universal salvation that is accessible only through Jesus Christ. This salvation underlines all phases of life including spiritual, physical, moral, material, mental, intellectual and economic areas. The authentic church provides relief in distress, healing in sickness and encouragement and prayer when facing tribulations, challenges and disasters of life. No Christian can rest on his laurels without following the example of the very author of Christianity, Jesus Christ. He dedicated his life to healing the sick, feeding the hungry, freeing those under the influence of Satan, relieving the suffering and deprivation of all kinds, assisting the poor, defending the oppressed and abused, and advocating for justice. God takes care of the whole person including mind, soul and body. He is interested in everything we do. He wants to meet our needs and work with us to help those around us. Beloved, I know that each one of us is very attached to his community, his company, his little world and his church, but the time has come to question everything because our eternal destiny is at stake. If the congregation that you love does not obey these basic teachings and these essential doctrines, it is worth taking another look.

Remember that Jesus was crucified for you. Make sure you are in harmony with what He said. Remember that only God gives eternal life. In fact He had to say, *"If someone comes to me, and he does not hate his father, his mother, his wife, his children, his brothers and sisters, and even his own life, he cannot be my disciple. And whosoever doth not bear his cross and follow me cannot be my disciple."* (Luke 14:25, 26). In other words, God must always take first place.

Sometimes the decision to obey and serve him isolates you and puts you on difficult terrain. Therefore he adds, *"I will not leave you orphans, I will come to you"* (John 14:18).

Hebrews 13:5 says, *"I will never leave you or forsake you."* **When we have God, we have everything we need. He is the most important at any time, any place and in whatever circumstances.** The decision to serve God is often harsh and drastic but necessary because it is for our eternal salvation.

I am personally convinced in the church of Jesus Christ that He will return to gather, as he promised in John 14:1-3, will not be called either Catholic or Anglican, Orthodox, or Lutheran, or Jehovah's Witnesses or Mormons or Church of Christ, or Philadelphia, or Baptist or Pentecostal or Presbyterian, or House of Yahweh, or Adventist or Episcopal, or Wesleyan or Family Radio, or Charismatic.

The Master of the universe does not consider what you know of monotheism, christology, polytheism, pantheism, or animism. He does not care about what degrees and qualifications you have in theology or philosophy or science. He is only coming for his dynamic and universal Church composed of believers who have maintained a close relationship with their God, who put into practice all that the Spirit enabled them to grasp and understand with all sincerity, and who have shown diligence in seeking the truth. Once this truth is received, it is accepted and implemented in their lives. Beloved, I beg you to continue to seek the truth with honesty and dedication. God searches the hearts and minds to see if you are genuine. I have no doubt He will lead you to the right path. Please, do not impose preconditions on him. Do not have prejudices. It would be illusory to believe that this will be easy. But, as PHILIPPIANS 4:13 states, *"I can do everything through Christ who strengthens me."*

The Faithful Mirror for The Authentic Church

"A man looks at his natural face in a glass." JAMES 1:23

1. God's law as experienced through Jesus

Jesus' record of Christian instruction — the summary of his message — is found in his sermon on the mountain that Matthew related extensively in his book, especially the fifth chapter. The best way to walk into the footsteps of the Messiah is to analyze his life. The Bible states that He lived an exemplary life. In HEBREW 4:15 we read, ***"For we have not an high priest which cannot be touched with the feeling of our infirmities; but was in all points tempted like as we are, yet without sin."*** JOHN 8:46 states, *"Which of you convinceth me of sin? And if I say the truth, why do ye not believe me?"* In other words, his attitude, which was reflected in his submission to the will of God by obeying him in everything, included supporting the sustainability of God's law.

In MATTHEW 5, He reveled his attitude toward the Law. That is to say, he came to give its proper interpretation, far from the excesses, traditions and Commandments of men. His contemporaries hated him for his approach and interpretation. He came to emphasize the transforming power of love that shapes our attitude instead of seeking for ways to make the conditions on this earth more difficult for mankind. He came to fulfill the statement found in JEREMIAH 31:33, *"I will put my law within them, and write it in their hearts, and I will be their God, and they shall be my people."*

It is important to realize that the transforming power of love that cannot continue indefinitely in one direction. Indeed, when we consider the sacrifices that the Host of heaven went through to save us, we cannot remain indifferent to such love. Thus was born a new approach that gave priority to the impulses of the heart instead of the rigid customs, traditions, rituals, and routines of the systemic priesthood.

2. God's law as interpreted by Jesus

Jesus Christ gave us the true interpretation of the law. In MARK 12:29-31, He summarized the Ten Commandments into two.

- The first is to love God above all.
- The second is to love our neighbor as ourselves.

This action does not repeal the Ten Commandments. In reality it presents our obligations to God in the first four Commandments and our relationships with others in the remaining six. Jesus said in MATTHEW 5:17-20 that He did not come to abolish the law but to fulfill it. In other words, as the authentic author, He was fully able and qualified to give the true interpretation of the Decalogue. Some say that the Ten Commandments have been abolished. If we are sincere and we want to respect the Bible, we cannot accept such a statement. Not only is it not biblical, but it defies logic. God is perfect. He knows everything, He sees the end from the beginning. He cannot give one thing today and later on turn around and say 'Oops ! Excuse me I made a mistake, let me change things around.' No! 1 SAMUEL 2:3 says, *"The Lord is the God who knows all."* MALACHI 3:6 says, *"I am the LORD, I change not."* What many call changes in reality are the gradual adjustments that the Lord makes based on the evolution of the maturity of mankind, but none of those reflect his character. If we read that God changed his mind about doing this or that or destroying nations or people, we must remember that God's mercy prevails. EZEKIEL 33:11 says *"As I live, says the Lord God, I have no pleasure in the death of the wicked but that the wicked turn from his way and live."* The Lord is always looking to save, not to destroy. When he makes certain declarations, it is to warn us, the sinners, to repent or pay the consequences for his or her sins. The word 'repent' does not really apply to God, but it is a human way to translate the fact that the results are conditional and based on what human beings choose to do. The foundation of God's government does not undergo changes. No government can function without some core principles that govern and define its relationships with the people. It is through those principles and those laws that order, stability, peace and security can flourish and those who disobey can be punished accordingly.

Indeed in ROMANS 3:20, Paul says, *"... by the law is the knowledge of sin."* In ROMANS 2:12, 13 we read, *"For as many as have sinned without law shall also perish without law: and as many as have sinned in the law shall be judged by the law; For not the hearers of the law are just before God, but the doers of the law shall be justified."* If we are truthful, we can see that even those who say the law is abolished, do not condone practices such as the worship of false gods, graven images, and the use of God's name in vain, disrespect of parents, murder, adultery, theft, deceit and greed. Let us be sincere with ourselves. If the law was abolished, why do they condemn such actions? We must be consistent. Let's be honest! The real point of contention regarding God's Ten Commandments concerns the fourth commandment that deals with the day of rest. **Is it Sunday or Saturday or any day?**

3. The saving grace of God's Law

The apostle Paul says in ROMAN 3:20-25. We need to know that nobody is justified before God by works of the law. Our salvation is obtained by grace. We are *"justified freely by his grace through the redemption that is in Christ Jesus."* (ROMANS 3:24). The redundancy necessary to emphasize the condition of salvation, *"justified freely by grace."* There should be no doubt among Christians that we are saved by grace. We graciously accept what Jesus offers us at a great price that none of us could ever pay. His blood and his death give us life. Therefore, common sense dictates a change of life. In Jesus Christ we become new creatures. So, do we still live in sin and practice a sinful existence? That is the question addressed by the apostle Paul in ROMANS 6:20. He goes overboard in ROMANS 14:8, stating that if we live, we live for the Lord. In GALATIANS 2:20 says, *"If I live, no longer I who live but Christ lives in me."*

Just imagine a young lady born into abject poverty. It is with great difficulty that she sometimes finds something to eat. She has no shelter, no clothes. She is in tatters. She is a lost case. Then one day, while living her miserable and mourned existence, a procession passed by her while she was on the sidewalk. In it were the country's prince and his dignitaries. Strangely enough, the procession stopped, the prince came out, stood up and greeted that poor young girl. She smiled timidly. He congratulated her for her beautiful smile. He invited her to follow him. She hesitated and said *"no way."* But the prince would not take no for an answer. He insisted. She told him how she was not worthy, not ready, and not clean. The prince did not budge. Finally, she got into the prince's limousine. She was shy and scared. She was afraid to even look at him furtively. To shorten the story, the prince wound up telleing her how much he loved her. He wanted to marry her. The girl was reluctant. With a little more persuasion, she thought she loved him too, but felt unworthy of such an honor. After many steps, dialogue, and persuasion, the girl eventually agreed. Then the great wedding of the land occurred. After becoming a princess, do you think she will return to her previous situation and lifestyle? She is expected to live as a princess. Naturally out of reciprocal love and especially gratitude, that princess will do her best to please her saving prince. She became a princess thanks to the magnanimity of the prince. Our attitude toward Jesus must be the same. Romans 5:8 says, *"While we were yet sinners, Christ died for us."* 2 Corinthians 5:21 says *"He who knew no sin he made to be sin for us so that we might be made the righteousness of God in him."*

4. Obedience to God through His Law

Because we are saved by grace, as proof of our love, we choose willingly to obey him. Since the law reflects his character, we strive to do what pleases him by obeying his commands. Jesus himself says in John 14:15, *"If you love me, keep my Commandments."* Naturally, no one can by himself obey God's law. James 2:10 says, *"Whosoever shall keep the whole law, and yet offend in one point, he is guilty of all."* In Romans 7:21, Paul reported the following, "*...when I would do good, evil is present with me.*" However, he could say in 2 Timothy 4:7, "*I have fought a good fight, I have finished my course, and I have kept the faith: Henceforth there is laid up for me a crown of righteousness, which the Lord, the righteous judge, shall give me.*" Or, "*I can do everything through him who strengthens me.*" (Philippians 4:13). Confused? Allow me this simple analogy.

I remember when my daughter was small and walking around. Everywhere I went, she wanted to go, too. Often when I had to go to drop the letters into the mail box at the post office, she would want to do it. She was small, so I would lift her up, open the box for her and she would drop the envelopes. She was so proud of herself with her big innocent smile, and I would say 'Bravo', but I did it all or the most important parts, taking her there, and opening the box. She was willing and had a great attitude. This is what the Lord wants from his people. What makes the difference for Paul, as well as for us, is our attitude. If we are docile, if we act in good faith, if we are obedient, and if we are sincere, the Lord who sees everything and knows everything will do the rest. He will compensate for our deficiencies. Otherwise, make no mistake, God cannot tolerate rebellion or cockiness. In 1 Samuel 15:22, he declares through his prophet Samuel, "*Obedience is better than sacrifice.*" Mockery, disobedience, irresponsibility, and the spirit of contention in a child would irritate any responsible parent, but if the child tries and obeys, every reasonable parent is willing to show compassion and understanding for his shortcomings and may even be willing to help him. God is our Father. Furthermore, He can see our attitudes and knows all our secrets. He does not like it when people play smart with Him. King Saul tried to pull a fast one by Him by playing smart. In 1 Samuel 16:1, God said to Samuel about Saul, *"I have rejected him."*

The Lord of the universe does not tolerate backsliding, cunning, or rogue behavior. Since we want to follow Jesus, let us come up clean in front of him with a humble spirit. If we must follow Jesus Christ, it is crucial that we regard this aspect of His life. This is how we can manifest our love for Him.

5. **Sabbath — the core of God's law**

a- Observation of the true day of rest.

What was Jesus Christ's attitude vis-à-vis the Ten Commandments, and specifically the fourth Commandment? According to Matthew 19:17, Jesus states: *"If thou wilt enter into life, keep the Commandments."* In the Christian world, the utterance of the word Sabbath makes people uncomfortable, to say the least. This is an extremely sensitive — if not volatile — subject that brings about contentious discussion, but if we have a minimum of good faith, with Jehovah as our witness, why should we be scared to hear or read what someone has to say about this thorny but vital issue? What are we afraid of?

I am glad that you, the reader, are willing to read the argument thoroughly, at least for intellectual knowledge. I approach this subject with great respect for each reader, whatever his or her position is. Sincerity requires us to admit that if we take all the Ten Commandments, all the explanations given for or against the Decalogue involve the fourth Commandment, namely the Sabbath.

Let us confront it without passion and with our heads over our shoulders and a lot of prayers. Everything is already said, this is a little reminder.

Note that no single denomination has the paternity of the Sabbath. But if history teaches us correctly, among the Christian religions, the *Seventh Day Baptists* were ahead among the contemporary religions to observe the Sabbath. Other churches have accepted it a little later. It is not a source of glory or pride for any single assembly. It is God's grace. Jesus claims ownership of the Sabbath when he declared in MATTHEW 12:8, "*The Son of Man is Lord even of the Sabbath.*" Nobody has a monopoly on the Sabbath. The Sabbath was made for man, according to Jesus in MARK 2:27. Other churches have adopted the Sabbath.

b- Which day is the 'true' day of rest?

Let's start by defining the word 'Sabbath'. Of Hebrew origin, it means 'rest'. This word is used for the first time in GENESIS 2:1-3 to express the memorial of creation. After creation, creatures should worship the Creator and recognize their dependence on him. It is a blessed day, sanctified or set apart for a special purpose. Human logic can lead us to ask ourselves, did the Creator need to rest? Was God tired? The Bible gives us a definite answer. God is never tired, according to ISAIAH 40:28. He did it for close communion with man and to receive the adoration of man. In his omniscience, he knew that man would need a change of activity to help him in various ways, including mentally and spiritually. Note that the Sabbath is mentioned before sin. The Sabbath is the final touch and final point to seal the creation of one week in which each day has 24 hours (In Hebrew, 'day' is translated as 'Yom', meaning a literal 24 hour period of time. There was evening, there was morning: GENESIS 1:5, 8, 13, 19, 23 and 31). We cannot honestly put the Sabbath in the lot of the ceremonial laws because God set it way before the introduction of sin into the world. The spirit of discernment and good faith can help us see the need to avoid mixing these concepts and confusing the minds of well-intentioned people who trust us to interpret the Bible properly. We need to put aside our 'little person' and the centuries of tradition and philosophy and to let God reign in us. Curiously, He can use anyone to show us something that may skip our bright intellect. You and I know that God is omniscient. He knows everything and sees the end from the beginning. *"I do not break my covenant and I will not change what came out of my lips."* (PSALMS 89:35). We change our minds when we are caught unprepared by lack of wisdom, planning or foresight. Is this the case for Jehovah? We know that the answer is *no*. Who was present after the creation? GENESIS 2:1-3 points out the presence of the Creator and Adam and Eve. What does Jesus tell us in MARK 2:27, 28? *"And he said unto them, The Sabbath was made for man, and not man for the Sabbath: Therefore the Son of man is Lord also of the Sabbath."* He said that the Sabbath was made for man. Jesus himself is the Lord of the Sabbath.

c- The rest of Sabbath before sin.

Was there any question of Adventist, Baptist, and Pentecostals in the beginning? Was there any question of Jews? Was there any question of sins? Was there any question of sacrifices? Was there any question of ceremonial activities? The answer is clearly no. Our first parents had not sinned yet when they had to deal with the issue of Sabbath. Besides, who created all things? Let's read JOHN 1:1-3 and HEBREWS 1:1-3 to confirm that it is Jesus, God the Creator who appears on earth to save mankind. When man disobeyed, God was not caught unprepared or by surprise. We recognize that the coming of sin into the world caused upheaval. However, certain facts have not changed, including the cycle of the week after the flood. Consult GENESIS 8:10-12, GENESIS 29:27 and we understand that this major disaster for the whole earth, did not alter the cycle of seven days of the week. With the Israelites, we have the formal resumption of theocratic relations. From DEUTERONOMY 4:13, DEUTERONOMY 5:22, EXODUS 34:28, EXODUS 31:18, versus DEUTERONOMY 4:14, our intelligence and our good faith help us to see a marked difference between the **Decalogue and the Mosaic laws**. The wording of the law that God gave the Jewish people is written by 'the finger of God' but the rest is written by Moses as dictated by God. It makes a big difference. When Moses broke the first two tablets of the law that God wrote of his 'finger', God could have said, *Child, you broke it you write it the second time*. Or He could have said *my dear Moses, I was about to abolish them, a little later, anyway. Don't worry! It's okay that you broke them*. No! Once again God took the care and time to rewrite them with 'his finger'. Why was it so? In EXODUS 20:1-17 we read the Decalogue. In EXODUS 20:8, the fourth commandment begins with the word 'remember'. This means that God did not establish the Sabbath for Jews at Sinai, but instead immediately after all things were created (GENESIS 1:31, 2:1). For the people of Israel, it was a reminder because while in slavery they could not observe the Holy Sabbath as God wanted them to do.

d- The Sabbath: A sign of eternal gratitude to God.

What reason did God give the people to observe the Sabbath? According to DEUTERONOMY 5:12-15, it was in recognition of his creative, liberating and redemptive power, an undeniable and a united power. The Bible expresses the promise that God made to the observers of the Sabbath in ISAIAH 58:13, 14. JEREMIAH 17:24-26 says, ***"And it shall come to pass, if ye diligently hearken unto me, saith the LORD, to bring in no burden through the gates of this city on the Sabbath day, but hallow the Sabbath day, to do no work therein;*** *Then shall there enter into the gates of this city kings and princes sitting upon the throne of David, riding in chariots and on horses, they, and their princes, the men of Judah, and the inhabitants of Jerusalem: and this city shall remain for ever. And they shall come from the cities of Judah, and from the places about Jerusalem, and from the land of Benjamin, and from the plain, and from the mountains, and from the south, bringing burnt offerings, and sacrifices, and meat offerings, and incense, and bringing sacrifices of praise, unto the house of the LORD."*

The same Bible, in the same chapter of JEREMIAH 17:27, also speaks of the punishment reserved for those who do not sanctify the Sabbath, ***"But if ye will not hearken unto me to hallow the Sabbath day, and not to bear a burden, even entering in at the gates of Jerusalem on the Sabbath day; then will I kindle a fire in the gates thereof, and it shall devour the palaces of Jerusalem, and it shall not be quenched."*** Do you mean to tell me that the insistence made by God from creation and throughout the Bible was only temporary? Read EXODUS 25 and you will see that when God commanded Moses to build him a tent, he took care to say in verse 9, *"you will make the tabernacle and all its utensils after the model I'll show you."* Also read Hebrews 8 and 9.

What was inside the tabernacle? According to Hebrews 9, especially verse 4, the tablets of the covenant were in there, too. So if the tent is built according to the model that God revealed to Moses, we can believe that the covenant is present in the real sanctuary.

e- The Sabbath as observed in the wilderness by the Israelites.

Under Jewish theocracy in the desert, we have an example in Numbers 15:32-36 that is terrifying to some and irritating to others. If we place the text in its appropriate context, we understand that God wanted to show the people the importance of the Sabbath. Better yet, he wanted to teach the children of Israel the importance of obeying the divine injunctions. This new generation that had just been freed from slavery needed to be well guided to begin and maintain relationships with God. They had as templates the Egyptians who served many gods. They learned to imitate their former masters. Generally, when people come out of bondage they tend to misinterpret the meaning of freedom and want to rest and have fun devoid of any responsibility or restriction to enjoy their emancipation. Reality demands that we be responsible citizens who obey the injunctions for civic and moral survival of any new nation or group of people recently freed from slavery. Once freed from the Egyptians, the people did not take long to want to express their freedom. The people were naturally rebellious. The Lord said in Exodus 32:9 that *"this people is a stiff-necked people."* They wanted to do as they pleased. God stepped in to avoid any misunderstanding. As evidence we can cite their attitude regarding the recommendations for manna. Indeed, when we read the Bible, especially Exodus 16:4, 5, Exodus 16:16-19, and Exodus 16:22-30, we see that the people chose to disobey by taking more or less than what was indicated, or by fetching the manna on the Sabbath, contrary to the specific order given. God took care of them by instructing them about how to observe the Sabbath (Exodus 16:23, Isaiah 58:13, 14).

They had to unlearn pagan traditions and learn how the true God should be served, not like the other false gods. The authentic knowledge of God is revealed in a progressive manner. Recall the example of Ananias and Sapphira in the New Testament. He had to use an example to set the tone for the new assembly. Now, people do whatever they want but not with impunity. If nothing happens to them, it is because we are approaching the time of the end where the final decision is at hand. In that time, he had to set examples. Otherwise everyone would do whatever they felt like doing and it would be plain anarchy. Remember the distinction between the Sabbath and the covenant. Exodus 34:27 speaks of the alliance in general, but Exodus 34:28 deals with the Sabbath and the Ten Commandments. Those who have a minimum of good faith, and discernment can see the difference. The covenant between God and the people includes the essential principles of justice or civil rights. In this same covenant was the Ten Commandments written by 'the finger of God'.

f- The ceremonial Sabbaths:
BEFORE the coming of the Messiah.

Like all nations, the Jews had parties and festive celebrations. The Gentiles had their own with a pagan character. The Jewish people of God, also had their feasts, but with socio-religious character. What happens on holidays? Generally there is no formal work, and people rest, and enjoy themselves. Do you remember how we translate 'rest' in the Jewish language ? Sabbath. Therefore, the Jewish people not only had the weekly Sabbath day of worship that God has called every man from Adam and Eve from creation to observe, but also every holiday was a holiday called Sabbath. Therefore, these holidays were also designated as 'Sabbaths' (days off). We can cite, for example EZEKIEL 46:1. These holidays also could fall and coincide with the weekly Sabbath. When that happens, that day has special meaning, like when Independence Day in the U.S., July 14 in France, or January 1st in Haiti, falls on a Sunday giving a double holiday in one day. When that happened for the Jewish people, it was a call for a double celebration.

g- The ceremonial Sabbaths: AFTER the coming of the Messiah.

These Jewish holidays include the Feast of Unleavened Bread, Pentecost, the Feast of Trumpets, the Day of Atonement and the Feast of Tabernacles, etc. Check LEVITICUS 23 for more information. These celebrations followed the lunar calendar. They could arrive any day of the week including coinciding with the weekly holy Sabbath. When this happened, according to JOHN 19:31, it became a 'great day', so the ceremonial laws of which everyone speaks also included the annual Jewish feasts that consisted of rituals and ceremonies, instituted at Mount Sinai. This law was commonly known as the law or the laws of Moses. These laws foretold the coming of Messiah. The observation of the majority of these annual celebrations, sacrifices and holocausts ended with the death of Jesus Christ on the cross.

Therefore, when Jesus expired on the cross, we read in LUKE 23:44-49 that a few things happened immediately, including the fact that the temple veil was torn, eliminating the separation between the holy place and the most holy place and the need for sacrifices, because 'the Lamb of God' was sacrificed once and for all. It is also in the light of such knowledge that Paul could declare in COLOSSIANS 2:16,17, ***"Let no man therefore judge you in meat, or in drink, or in respect of an holyday, or of the new moon, or of the Sabbath days:*** *Which are a shadow of things to come; but the body is of Christ."* Taking a minute to pray and to think on it, added to a minimum of common sense and good faith will allow us to understand the text. The apostle declares what any genuine Christian knows already. Was it not Jesus himself who said, *"Judge not that ye be not judged"* (MATTHEW 7:1). Only God can judge us. Do not judge people because they are not doing what you want or what you are doing. They are accountable to God. But, bear in mind if you are not allowed to judge me, it does not necessarily mean I am right. The apostle continued by declaring that Christ's death accomplishes everything that the sacrifices prefigured. They were announcing the upcoming of the Messiah. Clearly by confession and profession of faith we are Christians.

Christians believe in Christ and follow his example. According to 1 CORINTHIANS 8:6, HEBREWS 1:1, 2, and JOHN 1:3, Christ is the Creator. 1 JOHN 2:6, and

1 Peter 2:21 invite us to follow the example of the Master.

h- Jesus, the true Sabbath keeper.

Among the example that Jesus gave us — but many fail to grasp — it is his attitude toward the Sabbath. In the light of Luke 4:16, Mark 6:1, 2, Mark 1:21, and Mark 4:31, we see that Jesus used to enter the synagogue on the Sabbath. What formal statement did Jesus make there about the law? He did not come to abolish it but to perfect it, as in Matthew 5:17-19. In all human languages, 'to accomplish' does not mean to eliminate or abolish but to make more efficient and to improve. In Mark 2:28, 29, Jesus declared himself the Lord of the Sabbath. We cannot teach the author, the creator of one day, how to observe it.

i- Would Jesus have changed the Sabbath to Sunday?

Many say that the resurrection of Jesus on Sunday was a clear way to transfer the sanctity of the Sabbath to Sunday. To support the argument that the seventh day Sabbath was replaced by that of the first day, many cite Matthew 28:1, Mark 16:1, Luke 24:1, and John 20:1. They say that the English version has mistranslated Matthew 28:1, but in the original Greek it is clear that Saturday is replaced by Sunday. The answer is simply, no. We must silence our passions, and subdue our ego to allow the Holy Spirit to guide us in obedience. Sometimes, our great knowledge prevents us from seeing the obvious truth.

Just a simple question:

Is it possible that Jesus chose to rest in the tomb on the Sabbath day, to resume his life on Sunday morning? Why would a God so just leave this shadow of doubt cast over all Christians without ever mentioning such a change?

Some say that if Saturday was a day to rest after six days of labor, Sunday is their day to rejoice for the salvation provided by Christ's resurrection. We have no quarrel with that, if you want to respect the seventh-day Sabbath and then add another day to rejoice. That is fine, but do not claim that Sunday replace Saturday as the day of rest that God gave way before the introduction of sin into the world.

Some may say there are many unclear points, or mysteries in the Bible. I would agree with you, but by the same token I would challenge any sincere being to call the Sabbath obscure or mystery. It is very clear. GENESIS 2:1-3 stipulates that God created the world in six literal days of 24 hours, then he ended his work and rested on the seventh day. He blessed the seventh day, and sanctified it. This was way before the introduction of sin in the garden. Why did God bother to bless and sanctify the seventh day? Does that mean the other six days were not blessed or cursed?

Impossible, because everything was good and there was no evil then. He wanted to draw special attention to that day. That was the anniversary of his creation. Every seventh day, the anniversary was to be celebrated. Or could it be that in his omniscience, he wanted to do it that way because he knew that men would rebel against it? Isn't it strange that Sabbath and marriage, the two things that existed before sin are the most controversial these days?

All of us can agree that Jesus is the Truth, not a diplomat. He was never scared to tell the truth. Look at Matthew 15:12-14, Matthew 16:4, Matthew 21:45-46 and Matthew 23, and we have examples of his boldness. Don't you think he would have told them about the change in the Sabbath, if there was one? He scolded the Pharisees for adding burdens to what God required. In Matthew 23:23, he told them what they should have done, without neglecting the other things they care about. Long before his death, in Matthew 24:15-20, addressing his beloved and speaking of the destruction of Jerusalem, Jesus said, *"Pray that this does not happen in winter time or a Sabbath day."* Why?

Do you want to tell me he was teasing them while he had plans to change the seventh day Sabbath into the first day? Had such a plan been conceived, there was at least more than one occasion when Jesus had the opportunity to tell the disciples about such a change. Instead, he urged them to pray so that the destruction of Jerusalem would not happen on the Sabbath when his children would be assembled in the same place of worship. God is just and he avoids all ambiguities. He is not the author of Big Bang. He speaks without equivocation. He knows what he is doing. When Jesus spoke of the destruction of Jerusalem, he knew that his people were going to continue to observe the Sabbath. To the contrary, calamities happen to them because of their disobedience. He is omniscient and he knew it would happen in the year 70 A.D., long after his resurrection. This means that Jesus knew that these disciples would continue to observe the biblical Sabbath even after his ascension. Did the disciples make any changes regarding the observation of the Holy Sabbath? One may speculate, but it will not be found in the Bible.

Some find that Jesus was not categorical on the Sabbath. Should he continue to repeat himself? God is free to choose to repeat or not to repeat an order. In Eden, for instance, He gave his order once not to eat the forbidden fruit. God is independent. He is Almighty. He can do what he wants when wants it and how he wants it. He always know what he is doing. He makes sure he gives you all the details the first time, then you make your decision and get the consequences of your choices. He rested the Sabbath day, right after creation. Because the people were in captivity, He took care to repeat it on Mount Sinai in Exodus 20:8 where he said, *"Remember the day of rest."* The rest is up to us.

j- Jesus and the fulfillment of the law regarding the Sabbath.

Jesus came to correct and remove the introduction of man-made cumbersome restrictions, customs which made the Sabbath a chore. He said, *"It is lawful to do well on the Sabbath."* The change was not from one day to another but in the spirit in which the Sabbath was observed, that seventh day in the garden, that same seventh day He mentioned on Mount Sinai, that same seventh day in which Christ had the habit of going into the synagogue every week. Men had turned the holy day into a full burden by adding traditions and customs. **Jesus wanted to restore the original stature of the seventh day Sabbath, a day of delight, adoration and thanksgiving for all his children.**

First conclusions.

This is the same challenge we are facing in the 21st century. Salvation is offered to us only through Jesus Christ and not by the rituals and customs practiced, or our own meritorious actions, or even by observing the Sabbath. If anyone thinks he can merit salvation by obeying a specific commandment, he is wrong. If a religion or an organization requires the observation of any precept to be saved, it is far from the truth. Salvation is free for us all. Its cost is grace offered by Jesus Christ who died on the cross, paid the price to redeem us all. It is available, accept it. Once saved by grace, by an attitude of gratitude, the sincere Christian chooses freely to walk in the footsteps of Jesus, not to be saved but after being saved through Jesus. How can one claim to love someone and be grateful for what he has done and yet choose to ignore his will? We can accept what God says or disobey him. God does not sow confusion. God never insinuates doubt, and ambivalence. The enemy of our faith does that. He initiated this approach since Eden. Genesis 3:1 reveals that he went to Eve, saying, *"Did God really say?"* Even today, the same argument is being used, Did God really say that the Sabbath is a day of rest? People use all sorts of subterfuges or philosophies, or view-points to make us reason out our way and not obey God. Remember that with Jehovah, we do what he says 100 percent or we are wasting our time. Again, like any responsible parent, God has already spoken and he does not like to keep repeating himself like a demented old man. There are so many excuses and explanations out there that even sincere people are confused. The choice remains simple: obey God.

Sincerity is not enough to get us through. The rich young ruler in Mark 10 was sincere and Jesus loved him, but he did not go all the way because he could not let go of his worldly possessions. In other words, he chose his wealth over Jesus. *"If any man will come after me, let him deny himself, and take up his cross, and follow me"*, said Jesus in Matthew 16:24. When people have to decide regarding this issue, it is very difficult. Many do not know how to answer, or respond poorly. Let us remember that Satan had the nerve to dare Jesus by saying in Matthew 4:3, *"If you're the son of God …."* It is clear that the insinuation of doubt and confusion is not from God. God had already given the word. He even acted on it. Jesus observed the Sabbath every week while on this earth. He called himself the Sabbath Master. He rested the seventh day after creation. Even in the tomb he rested on the Sabbath and rose again on Sunday morning. We can make insinuations, deductions, become philosophers, and be tangential, but he has never told us to observe another day. We have never read that he specifically blessed another day. Let's be sincere! Man always wants to do whatever he wants and behaves according to his own rules. St. Paul says in Galatians 1:8, *"But when we ourselves, or an angel from heaven, preach any other gospel than the one we preached to you, they pose be anathema!"*

k - The disciples and the Sabbath after the death of Jesus.

After his resurrection, what did Jesus do on the first day of the week (Sunday)? In Mark 16:9, He appeared to Mary Magdalene. In Luke 24:33-43, He had an encounter on the road to Emmaus, before he went to share a meal with the disciples. The proponents for

Sunday say, *"here is proof that the disciples came together on a Sunday to commemorate the resurrection of Christ."* It would make much sense, but the disciples did not know that Jesus was resurrected. They were all in sorrow and fear. They took refuge in the upper room in dismay and did not recognize the risen Master who was among them, according to JOHN 20:19-21. When Jesus presented himself, they found it difficult to believe. How could they celebrate his resurrection? What did Joseph of Arimathea do on the day of the crucifixion? What did the women who had come from Galilee do? LUKE 23:50-56 tells us they put the body of Jesus in a tomb and then rested on the Sabbath, according to the law.

Is it reasonable to say that the Sabbath was the case of all contemporary Jews in Jesus' time? In light of the fourth commandment, they considered the declaration contained in EXODUS 20:8-11, *"thou shalt not do any work in this day."* Even in the case of the death of their beloved Jesus Christ, they chose to respect the Sabbath, and to go and anoint him at dawn on the first day. Then there are some who say that the change happened when Jesus rose. What did the ladies do on the first day of the week? LUKE 24:1 tells us that after having rested on the Sabbath, at dawn the first day they went into the tomb where Jesus was put to embalm him. Besides the immutable character of Jehovah, we have enough facts to refute with good conscience and calmness of mind those who claim that the seventh day Sabbath was replaced by the 'Sunday Sabbath' of the first day. This is only by deduction or inference or a figment of their imagination. Beloved, this is very important and requires intense discussions in humility and prayer for those who are serving God in good faith.

What happened after Jesus went to heaven? What was the attitude of the disciples after the ascent of Jesus Christ?

I- Paul and the Sabbath after the ascent of Jesus.

Take for example the Apostle Paul, the favorite among many who quote him often. What did he do?

Read: ACTS 13:13-16, 42-44; ACTS 16:16; ACTS 17:1,2; and ACTS 18:1-4, 11. These texts show us that every seventh day Sabbath, Paul went to church or sought a place to worship or teach. If there were real changes, it would be ideal for Paul to tell them. What was Paul doing the first day of the week? See ACTS 20:6-14. He was preparing for a journey to preach the gospel of the kingdom, but not to worship. What other things did Paul do on the first day? He invited the faithful to set aside the gifts at home from the first day. If one were to prepare the offering home from the first day, the idea of preparation does not equate execution. The preposition 'from' the first day, does not give us the sense of achievement but a preparation for future cases. In 1 CORINTHIANS 16:1, 2, 'home' is equivalent to the Greek word *apes se*, not in church but at home. *Not in the collection plate at church*. According to the translation of the Vulgate and Castellio, it means 'At home, in his house'. The French version, Ostwald, Martin, KJV, and De Sacy, all give the same translation of 'put aside in his house'. In other words, the apostle Paul urged people to put aside their gifts at home since the first day to bring them to the worship service the seventh day. It is the only logical explanation. In light of these texts of Paul, we can explain COLOSSIANS 2:16, 17. Here it is the Sabbath, festivals, and ceremonial rest that are shadows of things to come. For once Christ died and rose again, he could satisfy all requirements to which the sacrifices and ceremonial festivities were necessary. The apostle Paul never included the seventh day Sabbath in this text. If so he would have revealed himself as inconsistent, hypocritical and in conflict with himself and what he believed, because the Bible revealed that he was attending services on the Sabbath regularly.

In conclusion: The Sabbath is deeply rooted in God's law.

Let us remember that the seventh-day Sabbath was created in Eden, before the advent of sin in creation. It is blessed by God himself. God reminded the Israelites about its holiness. It was observed by Jesus himself and the disciples. Why would Paul come along, out of the blue, to change, or include the seventh day Sabbath, created in Eden, before the advent of sin into the world, blessed by God himself, reminded to generations, and observed by Jesus himself? Why would Paul be the one authorized to put that holy Sabbath in the mix bag of ceremonial laws and services that Moses gave the people of Israel? Remember, even in Moses' time, he wrote the ceremonial laws, but when it came to the Ten Commandments, God wrote them himself with *"his own finger."* (EXODUS 31:18). Why was God so careful to make such a distinction? Even after Moses broke the first set, God again wrote the second set. Why? How could Paul change what Moses could not even write?

Why say that the law is abolished and at the same time tacitly observe nine of the Ten Commandments, except the fourth? James 2:8 mentions that observing nine out of ten means nothing. This does not mean we can observe them all by our own strength, but to choose deliberately to put one aside is not acceptable to God. We need to be consistent and sincere with ourselves. If the law is abolished, we cannot speak of sin because sin is the *"transgression of the law"*, according to 1 John 3:4. Do you think God can make a world so complex without laws? Would you live in a country without laws? Again, salvation is free only by accepting Jesus Christ. Paul says, *"Bring forth therefore fruits worthy of repentance."* The child of God is not saved by law. However, being saved by grace, he strove to please his God by obeying him.

We also can explain what Paul meant in Galatians 4:10, 11 or Philippians 3:17. *"Be imitators of me as I myself am of Christ."* or again as "*... myself, I continue to imitate Christ.*"

Even if an angel announces another gospel, let it be anathema! You want to say that despite the fact that Jesus could have changed the Sabbath to Sunday and did not, the disciples, including Paul, were going to do the opposite and still observe the Sabbath? Intellectual integrity, the moral compass each one of us has, allows us to agree on one fact, the change of the Sabbath to Sunday is — at most — a case of deduction or shy innuendo. As for continuing with the seventh day Sabbath, the facts remain solid and overwhelming. It is clearly said to observe the seventh day Sabbath. We see Jesus and the disciples themselves observe the seventh day Sabbath unequivocally. What example would a sincere believer choose? The choice is simple, even easy- what everyone does, or what is stipulated in the Bible?

"Those who say Lord, Lord, will not all enter in the kingdom of heaven, but the one who does the will of my Father in heaven." (MATTHEW 7:21).

Again Jesus warns us not to follow the crowd. In 1 CORINTHIANS 4:20, Paul tells us that the kingdom of God does not consist in words but in deeds. MATTHEW 7:13 gives us another solemn reminder from Jesus Christ, *"Enter through the narrow gate. For wide is the gate and is the path that leads to destruction, and there are many who enter through it."*

Be careful. Remember the text inserted in 2 THESSALONIANS 2:11 that some receive a strong delusion to believe a lie. Be careful not to be among those who share this spirit of bewilderment. We add that to continue to resist the force of truth is contradictory to being a believer. It is counter productive. Woe to us if we learn to reason or wiggle our way out to avoid obedience to divine injunctions, thinking He will accept our maneuvers. There comes a time, after resisting the truth for so long, that we become naturally fond of lie that draws us constantly while truth is avoided. We may welcome whatever keeps us comfortable in our situation, although we are outside of the authentic faith that saves. Between faith and presumption, there is less than a step. People can be mistaken easily to think of being on the right track. ROMANS 1:22 states that many people who profess themselves as wise have become fools.

Let us always remember that salvation is a heavenly favor. However, after being saved, it is polite to want to know what is pleasing to God, not to earn salvation, but as a tribute to this great salvation. Be careful not to fall into the trap of 'ad hominum fallacy', that is to be looking for excuses to dethrone what is crucial in reasoning. How many times people avoid talking about the authenticity of the Sabbath, and prefer remarks such as, *"observers of the Sabbath lack of love, are proud, or have a prophetess, etc."* This is not the issue that is being discussed now. We can talk about that on another occasion. But for now let us be of good faith, accept the truth and strive to put it into practice, even if we are in the minority.

Some may still have doubts, so, I present the following scene to illustrate this point: Considering the attributes of God that define him, including his fairness and justice, imagine the following example: two sincere believers adopt two different attitudes.

Believer # 1 knows he is saved by grace. Being saved without any contribution from him, he does his best to show his gratitude by obeying his Redeemer. He continues to worship on Sunday.

Believer # 2 is also convinced that only the blood of Jesus Christ shed on the cross gives him access to the eternal kingdom of glory. He said that in light of the Bible, he is part of the minority who observes the Sabbath on the seventh day.

The day of reckoning arrives. Both come and stand before the throne of God for the trial. In his righteousness, what argument will carry more weight for the Creator? If God asks them to support their decision for Sunday or Saturday, without inference, deduction or bent, just the biblical texts, which one would be in a better situation? What action should we take? Everyone must make a decision. Remember that we can pull up a biblical text to support the majority of our positions, but is it taken within its context? Are we in harmony with the Bible or are we using all kinds of techniques to convince ourselves to do away with what is truly said, just because it is uncomfortable? We also find that some texts are a bit difficult and ambiguous, in this case we need to show good faith and let the Holy Spirit guide us. Remember God's attributes. Ask God to guide us but do not summon him to change what he has said in order to accommodate us. Do not say, *"most people are doing it."* EXODUS 23:2 God said *"Thou shalt not follow a multitude to do evil."* It takes more than pure human reasoning, because God's reasoning is based upon basic principles that are part of his character. It takes more than being genuine. It requires diligence to seek, find the truth and obey it. If we need to err, let it be in good faith not because of personal biases or preferences. Let us be docile in the hands of the Creator and He will guide us if we are sincere. The trouble is that often we are inclined to follow parents, friends, church leaders, tradition, myths, and the influence of Greco-Roman sophistry to model ourselves according to the stands of the majority without knowing it. The Bible is replete with examples where the majority was wrong. Let us watch and pray! I understand that the beliefs or dogmas transmitted to us by our parents or the church have taken root within us already. This is the result of several generations. For many, it is very difficult to abdicate now, but I remind you the experience of Paul who did not hesitate to turn back once he realized he was heading in the wrong direction. He did not make any excuses. Zeal, good faith, good conscience and sincerity are not enough to avoid falling into error. The Most High tells us in several ways. However, our prejudices and our tendency to anticipate how God operates makes us blind, and hardens our understanding. Saul of Tarsis, who later on became Paul, was a man who did his best to serve God. He was sincere and devoted, but he was wrong. When he received the strange truth that the Christian minority church he was persecuting was the one holding the salvific truth, while all institutions and legitimate religious authorities, to which he belonged was wrong, he had to take a stand for truth or for the majority. It was a painful choice. But Paul realized he could not resist the heavenly vision. The day will come when a lot of us will have to abdicate. It may be too late for salvation but time for judgment and condemnation. Fortunately, the good news is that you and I can still choose to obey and please God now, as Paul decided to do his will without further tossing and turning. I hope that you had the courage to read these lines. I hope you are seriously thinking about your personal position of obedience or disobedience before God and his word. May you choose to obey the Creator! If this simple analysis on the word of God reaches your heart, do not be upset, but think seriously about your ultimate destiny. Before it is too late, will you decide for God and observe His law? The author of the book of HEBREWS 3:7, 8 invites us not to harden our hearts if we hear the voice of the Holy Spirit.

I am thinking of a friend of mine since childhood. She always believed that Sunday was the Sabbath until she realized that the 'Sabbath on Sunday' was an institution set up by clever men and human dignitaries. Did she change? Did she choose to worship God on the seventh day Sabbath? No. For a long while she refused to do so, arguing that she prefers to follow the footsteps of her parents and grandparents, and obey the laws of her church.

By doing so, she seemed to have rejected God's law for the comfort of her environment. According to ACTS 5:29, "*We must obey God rather than men.*" To avoid straining the relationship, I said, "*as I am getting older I am more and more tempted to adopt February 29 as my birthday. That way I could reduce my calendar years. But no matter how hard I try, the years will pile up and I can never change the day my mother gave birth to me.*" There are certain dates we cannot change. GENESIS 2:2, 3 states that, "*On the seventh day God ended his work which he had made; and he rested on the seventh day from all his work which he had made. And God blessed the seventh day, and sanctified it: because that in it he had rested from all his work which God created and made.*" The seventh day is the anniversary of God's creation. We may try to change it, but certain dates or days can never be changed truly. She would not budge. Although I did not share her views, I respected her position. We remained friends. I did my job in good conscience. We did not become bitter over it. I cannot describe my happiness when 3 years ago she called me to give me the good news that she decided to observe the true seventh day Sabbath. All of us must do our best and let God do the rest. My last urge was not only to respect her decision, but also to remind her that salvation is through grace and not through our deeds.

The call to obey is given to all. Unfortunately, all will not respond. "*Many are called but few are chosen.*" MATTHEW 22:14). The choice is personal.

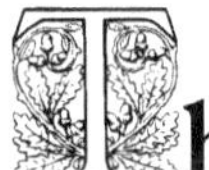he Essence of Life: Choosing

In the 21st century, man is defined in terms of molecular biology, physiology and thermodynamics. In other words, he is seen through genetic data that support him such as DNA / RNA, the maintenance of competing biochemical reactions that occur in him, and his ability to draw energy from his environment in order to self perpetuate, transform and improve on himself.

In ancient times, it was a little more sentimental. Several thinkers, including Epicurus, wanted to define man according to their observation and personal experience. For them, there is a natural tendency to avoid anything that can cause pain and discomfort, and to embrace whatever can procure pleasure and happiness. We must admit that everyone's life span is relatively short and people try to define it by pursuing happiness and avoiding pain. Unfortunately, in the biological sphere the steps taken to reach the desired goals often wind up producing the wrong result. This led some philosophers, including Rene Descartes, Baruch Spinoza and Jeremy Bentham to postulate that happiness is a mirage or an unattainable ideal. They believed that pleasure and pain are part of a continuum that involves the path of neurotransmitters such as dopamine and endorphins. Pascal, for his part, said that happiness is impossible to man. All in all, the decision is not unanimous and the jury is still out. Everything continues to be questioned. Whether scientist, philosopher, or theologian, one is forced to admit that the compendium of life is based on the key principle of **choice**, action.

Even the Bible supports such an approach. We read in GENESIS 2:16,17, ***"And the LORD God commanded the man, saying, Of every tree of the garden thou mayest freely eat:*** *But of the tree of the knowledge of good and evil, thou shalt not eat of it: for in the day that thou eatest thereof thou shalt surely die."*

Of course choosing and acting have prerequisites, including maturity, good judgment, and the ability to understand, analyze and weigh the consequences. Genesis underscores not only that Adam understood the order given, but he also could choose to obey or disobey with the result clearly explained. According to GENESIS 4:7, God said to Cain, ***"If thou doest well, shalt thou not be accepted? and if thou doest not well, sin lieth at the door. And unto thee shall be his desire, and thou shalt rule over him."*** JOSHUA 24:15 says, *"Choose today whom you will serve."*

DEUTERONOMY 30:19 says, *"I have set before you life and death, blessing and curse. Therefore choose life, that you may live, thou and thy seed."* Allow us to infer that life and blessings are translated as happiness; death and curse reflect unhappiness. Whether we like it or not, our life is defined by our choices. Besides, we repeat all the time that 'life is a choice' or 'life is action'.

In the spiritual realm of options usually the challenge is not in the idea of choosing itself. We are aware of what to choose. The difficulty arises in acting, following through, taking the proper steps and making the right selection. According to the spiritual teaching,

God invites us to choose between good and evil, life and death, light and darkness, and truth and error. The Israelites became very accustomed to this kind of education. Jesus himself used that same approach during his rabbinical ministry. In LUKE 16:13, he stated, *"No servant can serve two masters. For either he will hate the one and love the other, or he will hold to the one and despise the other. You cannot serve God and Mammon."*

Mammon is the Greek word 'Mammon' and in Aramaic, 'Mammon'. It means money, personification of wealth, the god of earthly things. This is the most effective way for the enemy to cause the destruction of the human race.

From Eden on, God has avoided any ambiguity in addressing humanity, but the enemy of our souls has invented what we call the nuances, the gray area of 'a little bit', 'not quite', 'It depends', 'not so strict', or 'not so stiff', 'avoid being so intolerant', 'let's not panic', 'avoid the forbidden frustration that can make us sick', and 'It's one life to live'. This is how our world sees things. No need to be strict or serious about anything.

In reality, the old principle — the two ways principle — the right way on the one hand and the back door, tortuous and dangerous way on the other hand should still apply. Now, nothing is absolute. It depends on the interpretations. The important thing is that we have fun and enjoy life. The definition that our world gives of freedom is being able to do whatever you want, whenever, wherever and with whomever you want, without restriction and without regard to consequences. Everything is relative. We live in the time of gray areas, compromises, and alternatives. God said not to eat of the tree of knowledge of good and evil, but the enemy said: "*Did God really say that? Maybe you misunderstood him. How can he limit your freedom. Doesn't he trust your judgment to make your own decision? How can you be free if you cannot do whatever you want.*" The Creator said, "*If you eat it you will surely die.*" The usurper said, "*ye shall not surely die, to the contrary, upon eating it your eyes shall be opened, and ye shall be as gods.*" (GENESIS 3:4,5). Our first parents should have remembered who their creator was, who worked diligently for their well being, and who did not. They decided to follow the devil, represented by the talking serpent that they did not know and that did not do anything for them. They ignored the orders of Yahweh who created them and provided them lavishly everything they could enjoy in the garden.

In GENESIS 4 we see Cain — controlled by Satan — who rebelled against the divine declarations to the point of initiating the first fratricide in human history. Today, God gives clear instructions about how he wants us to live. He speaks of eternal life or eternal destruction, and the enemy asks why not a purgatory or an eternal hell. In ACTS 4:12 God says that salvation is granted by Christ and Christ alone. The enemy says not so fast, why not go through Mary, the saints, indulgences, works, religion, some other names, or even under the umbrella of some specific organizations? God promulgates the Ten Commandments, including the 4th, but men try to play it smart. Sometimes they say the law has been abolished or sometime they claim that Jesus Christ changed it after his resurrection on a Sunday, or no one knows which day is the seventh day, so why not Sunday, Friday or any day. Yet another argument is that "*I am a Christian but God sees that the leaders are bad, so let me stay home in communion with myself and my God. He sees it all, He will accept me home because he understands everything."*

God created Eve for Adam to make a couple. Today we say, I can choose any one and as many as I want. God says to love your neighbor who is closest. We say why not the one I choose to love because he or she yields to all my wishes.

God says take care of his church, we begin to reason — people do not make good use of my money, things are difficult, God knows, I can better manage what I sweat to earn.

Jesus said in MATTHEW 6:34, *"Do not worry about tomorrow: for tomorrow shall take care of itself."* We add, as great thinkers, *"Heaven helps those who help themselves."* In other words, everyone should do his best, get the most and not worry about anyone else.

According to JOHN 3:16, salvation is granted to all who accept it. The great thinkers say that Jesus died only for a category of people and only for those who are saved.

Dear friends I must remind you that this tendency to contradict, correct, delete, reason, or add to the divine injunctions is from the devil. He will cause the majority of people to head straight to destruction. Wherever the path of the Lord is clearly indicated, the enemy introduces simple little nuances, innuendo, or a counterfeit. The cancer of doubt is making havoc in God's assembly. The devil finds a loophole or he initiates just a little crack or a little opening to spray his venom of doubt. Often, we forget that God pays close attention to details and our intent means much more than our words or deeds.

Jesus says in MATTHEW 5:37, let your word be yes, or no, whatever is between and unclear stems from evil.

An intelligent choice.

Willingly or unwillingly, we are influenced by the environment in which we operate. As Christians, we are caught in this tidal wave, the snare of the devil, because we have to live, we have needs, and our flesh and blood are consumed with desires. Nevertheless, throughout the Bible we are convinced of two facts.

a.) God always took care of the faithful. He delivered those who chose to obey the divine injunctions, even through the worst adversity. Indeed, the tests are the passport to reach the ultimate victory. Noah, Job, Abraham, Joseph, Moses, Joshua, Daniel, the apostles, and the martyrs are there to prove it.

b.) Those who disobeyed, paid the consequences, Adam and Eve, Cain, Lot, Kore, Dothan and Abiram, Balaam, King Saul and Ahab, Ananias and Saphira, Uzza and even Moses.

GALATIANS 6:7 says, *"Do not be fooled: we do not make fun of God. What that 'a man soweth, that shall he also reap"*.

Beloved, if we are really intelligent, we should yield to the Holy Spirit and strive to obey the divine voice. Let's stop the delaying tactics, the fruitless discussions, and the false arguments. In REVELATIONS 3:20, we read that Jesus is 'knocking at the door'. Dear friends, this is not normal. Jesus should not be knocking at the door.

He should be inside and dining with us as the Host of Honor.

The consequences of our choices

Jesus emphatically stated that we must make choices. Every moment we choose between:

- Dedicating ourselves to God for eternal treasure or
- Attaching ourselves to Mammon for his treasure.

Whether through our words, our actions or thoughts, our life and our eternal destiny revolve around that concept. It focuses on our choices. There is no getting away from it. The natural impulse in us will require us to decide whether to follow God or Mammon. To follow God is for the mind to reap eternal life. Serving Mammon is to plant for the flesh and the flesh reaps corruption, eternal destruction. We must be careful not to choose Mammon when we believe we have opted for God.

The Apostle James opened the fourth chapter of his book with questions such as, Where do the wars, the quarrels, animosities, jealousies, envy, ambition, intrigue, fierce attacks, and murders come from? Everything is based on the insatiable desire of man to have ever more, and especially more than the others around him and to be judged superior to others. There is nothing wrong with having money when it is acquired or earned properly and when it can be used for great deeds to help self, others and God's cause. It becomes a curse when people are willing to do anything to get it at any cost. Paul states in 1 Timothy 6:10, that the love of money is the root of all evil. Let's be honest, money can do extraordinary things for us and for God's ministry. The majority of our concerns and needs are legitimate and even essential to our survival. Can we imagine the amount of good that money can do for a community? All of us want a home, cars, comfort, clothing, entertainment, and this is achieved with money. God has a different approach. MATTHEW 6:33 says, *"Seek first the kingdom of God and His righteousness and all these things will be given unto you."*

MATTHEW 19:27-29 says, "*Then Peter answered him," Behold, we have left all and followed thee, what will he do for us? Jesus answered them, I tell you the truth, when the Son of man in the renewal of all things, sits on the throne of his glory, you who have followed Me will also sit on twelve thrones, judging the twelve tribes of Israel. And anyone who left because of my name, brothers, or sisters, or father, or mother, or wife, or children, or lands, or houses, will receive a hundredfold, and inherit life eternal. Several of the first shall be last, and the last shall be first.*" God wants us to realize he is the ultimate provider of everything.

Some tips to help us make the right choice.

If we want with all our hearts to serve the Master, some points need to be revisited:

1. Come to grasp with our condition without God, identify our attitude (our state of mind without bias), and realize the necessity to seek God's mercy.

2. Identify the priority order of our existence, accept the only way of salvation, Jesus Christ and beg him to have mercy on us.

3. Establish or restore our relationship with God. Read his word, obey Him faithfully and let Him manage our lives.

4. Acquire knowledge from God's word.

5. Pray for the Holy Spirit to help us discern truth from errors.

6. Pay attention to the needs of others and help them walk in faith.

The battle continues with Mammon.

Let us not be misled into believing that God has changed. JUDE 9 tells that the archangel Michael contending with the devil disputed the body of Moses, a man who was constantly in contact with God and to whom God spoke regularly. Satan had the nerve to want to claim his body. If that could happen to Moses, what will he hesitate to lay claim upon? We must always choose to be reconciled with the Most High and act on it right away.

Ultimately, we are engaged in a merciless war and the stakes are eternal life. We constantly choose between God and Satan. It is clear that God uses a different standard. If we are intelligent in choosing God, we win 'big time' not only in this world but also in the new one to come. Beloved, the Christian's life demands faith and commitment to choose and act appropriately. In LUKE 12:15 Jesus says, *"Keep yourselves from covetousness, for a man's life does not depend on his property, was there in abundance."* Are you intelligent? Do you truly believe? Then you should submit to the Lord's will. If we read and understand the scriptures, including 1 KINGS 17,

Luke 1:22, Matthew 6 and many other biblical passages, let us work together in God's vineyard.

In God's true Church, there should not be indigent or people who lack even the bare minimum to survive. All of us have different talents and levels of qualifications that can be put together to help everybody. Beloved, choosing God means having enough faith to give him everything and allow him to manage it as he sees fit. God's role depends on our willingness to surrender to him.

Salvation: Predestination vs. Personal choice?

According to Matthew 22:14, Many are called but few are chosen. In other words, a large crowd responds to the call, but very few make it.

Does this mean that God discriminates by picking and choosing? By examining Acts 10:34 *"Then Peter opened his mouth, and said, Of a truth I perceive that God is no respecter of persons"*, Romans 2:11, *"for there is no respect of persons with God."*, Colossians 3:25, *"But he that doeth wrong shall receive for the wrong which he hath done and there is no respect of persons."*, Hebrews 2:9, *"But we see Jesus, who was made a little lower than the angels for the suffering of death, crowned with glory and honor; that he by the grace of God should taste death for every man."*, 1 Peter 1:17, *"And if ye call on the Father, who without respect of persons judgeth according to every man's work, pass the time of your sojourning here in fear."*, 2 Chronicles 19:7, Galatians 2:6, Ephesians 6:9, etc., we consider the answer to be **No.**

Christ died for us all. All of us have become sinners in Adam and all of us have received grace in Jesus.

ROMANS 5:12 says, "*Therefore as by the offense of one judgment came upon all men to condemnation; even so by the righteousness of one the free gift came upon all men unto justification of life*". Therefore, salvation is available for everyone, but everyone has the option to accept or reject it.

The idea that God chooses a few and then leaves the rest for the lake of fire to burn eternally is not biblical. As a matter of fact, Jesus states clearly in MATTHEW 25:41 that the everlasting fire was prepared for the devil and his angels.

Unfortunately, many may not take advantage of the divine offer. God loves everyone but gives us the freedom to make our own choice. What many seem to misunderstand is God's ability to select people for a specific mission. When God chose Abraham, Moses, Jacob, and the Israelites, He did it within the frame of His power and His attributes to be just and merciful. He knows the character, skills, talents, and the gifts of everyone. He can select anyone he pleases to accomplish specific tasks.

This does not mean that he rejects others when it comes to their own personal salvation. He chose Jacob to be the father of all the Israelites, and rejected Esau for this specific goal. This does not mean that Esau was banned from being saved. He tried to get Cain to repent. When He chose the Israelites, it was for them to be a model to attract the other nations to Him, but the Israelites misunderstood and thought it was an exclusive right. They failed miserably. 1 TIMOTHY 2:4 states clearly that God wants salvation for all men, "*who will have all men to be saved, and to come unto the knowledge of the truth."* TITUS 2:11 states, *"For the grace of God that bringeth salvation hath appeared to all men."* God does not seek to punish anyone. He gives us all opportunities to be saved. Those who respond and found mercy in the Lord are not obsessed by the things of this world.

Who chooses the saved ones? The Lord of hosts, of course. **How does he choose his elect?** On what basis does he do it? He does not apply a capricious formula of predestination. We must recognize that God, in his prescience, sees the life's outcome of every human being in particular. He knows in advance who will persevere to the end until eternal life. When he conceived the plan of redemption *"before the foundation of the world,"* this does not mean he rejected the first Adam, but He knew that Adam would opt the disobedience, using his freedom of choice. In his love, he made ample provision for his restoration. JOHN 3:16 clearly states that Christ died to save everyone who believes in him.

Jesus wept over Jerusalem, not by hypocrisy, but because he really wanted to save the inhabitants of this city, the Jewish nation. The people willfully rejected him and opted for the status quo. They wanted to follow the system and the officials of the institution at the time. Another example is the parallel between the rich young man in MARK 10:17-27 and Saul of Tarsus on the road to Damascus (ACTS of the Apostles, chapter 9). That rich young ruler wanted to have everlasting life. Jesus himself looked at him, loved him, and wanted to save him. The young man had great possessions and he opted to stay with them instead of selling them off and giving the profits to the poor so he could then follow Jesus. This illustrates the basic principle that God can put everything in motion for our salvation, but he will not violate our will. Consider the case of Saul of Tarsus in the book of Acts, chapter 9. Paul was willing to persecute Christians to eliminate the new doctrine, Christianity. On the way to accomplishing his purposes, he received the call from heaven. His answer was a clear and simple, *"Lord, what wilt thou have me do?"* He turned around immediately and engaged body and soul to serve Jesus Christ wholeheartedly. He gave up fame, social status, position, promotion and a bright future in the system where he was. He accepted Christ and as a result his earthly bright future turned into a nightmare with contempt, persecution, ridicule and death. Between the rich young man and Saul of Tarsus, there is a key difference: If both received the call for salvation, Paul repented and submitted his will to the divine sovereignty, while the young ruler resisted Jesus Christ's appeal.

In accord with the spirit of the Bible, God has always wanted to restore all men. Ultimately, according to REVELATIONS 7, starting with verse 3, those who were saved through the blood of the Lord include representatives from the twelve Tribes of the Israelites, the twelve apostles, plus a great multitude which no man could number, of all nations and kindreds and people and tongues. What qualifies these people can be summarized in two steps:

1. They realize their sinful nature.
2. They amend, accept Jesus' sacrifice fully.

Those who are not saved, choose freely to do otherwise.

Ezekiel 33:11 says clearly that what God wants is not the death of the wicked, but that the wicked changes his ways and lives. God does not bluff. If he makes a statement, he knows how to apply the rules to back it up. Two robbers were crucified with Jesus Christ, one accepted him as the Christ, and salvation was promised. The other rejected and mocked him because he did not believe. Responsible parents can understand God's plan a bit easier. Many parents have an idea of the fate of their children, taking into account their tendencies, character, and attitudes, even as a child. Parents can do their best, but often these children yield to peer pressures and their own weaknesses and things turn sour. Also, a negative experience inside the church can affect the younger generation. This can torpedo their faith forever. This is why leaders must be very careful. Salvation is offered to all but many do not accept it. They deny the existence of God and their case is decided. Even in that group there is still a possibility, be it at the last minute, that some may sincerely repent, confess their sins, accept Christ as their personal Savior and be saved.

The road that leads to everlasting life.

Many want eternal life. Everyone wants a life of bliss for eternity, but it comes only by choosing God and acting on his promises. God made his election from what He knows, and sees that may not be humanly visible. Let us remember that *"Man looks at the outward appearance, but the Lord looks at the heart."* (1 Samuel 16:7). Even now, during this reading, God Himself searches the heart and innermost intentions. Everything is naked before him. Are we sincere, faithful, and committed enough to be among the elect, or are we in the majority that are called but will be disappointed for not having taken Him seriously enough, willing to leave everything, denying self, to serve Him? Let us remember the verses of MATTHEW 7:21-23, Jesus himself says, *"Those who say Lord, Lord! will not all be in the kingdom of heaven, but he that doeth the will of my Father in heaven. Many will say in that day to the Lord, Lord, did we not prophesy in Your name? Didn't we cast demons in Your name? And have we not done many wonders in Your name? Then I will declare to them I've never known you, do you get from me, you who practice lawlessness."* What a disappointment. It is often said that the road of *"Hell is paved with good intentions."* In other words, many delude themselves but will be among those who cry *"mountains fall on us."* How awful! Any regrets? What a loss.

Getting ready for everlasting life: the last stretch.

Have you ever had the privilege of visiting a military base where hundreds or thousands, of brave young men and women are trained to confront the nation's enemies? It is an experience to have. It fills you with pride to see young people deliberately choose to risk their lives to safeguard national sovereignty without being drafted. What great sacrifices they consent to — abandoning their parents, spouses, homes, and friends, waking up early every morning and staying up late at night, wearing uniforms, eating only what they are given, spending hours in all kinds of workouts daily, and subjugating their will to that of a chief, coupled with the possibility of dying on the battlefield. They gave up everything to serve their country.

What about the Christian army? Are there a few real soldiers choosing to fight against the common enemy? The disciple of Gamaliel said in

ROMANS 8:35-39, *"what can separate us from the love of Christ? Will tribulation, or distress, or persecution, or famine, or nakedness, or peril, or sword? … I am confident that neither death nor life, nor angels, nor principalities, nor things present nor things to come, nor powers, nor height nor depth, nor any other creature can separate us from the love of God revealed in Jesus Christ our Lord."*

It is my sincere wish that you and I search ourselves thoroughly and make the right choice for the everlasting reward provided by grace to all who accept it.

Epilogue

When one considers the abundance of literature on religion, in general, and the Bible in particular, choosing to write on such a popular subject is definitely a risk. I decided to take it for the love of my brethren. Furthermore, the position becomes increasingly difficult because I dare to speak about "the truth". Some believe that the absolute truth transcends the human domain and prefer to accept a truth that depends on the person who defines it and those who hear it. We tend to see the truth according to our own suggestive convictions. In religion, truth has become synonymous with popularity, wealth, eloquence, and using the techniques learned to play on the emotions and bring the crowd to its feet. It is in this skeptical and materialistic environment, in the 21st century, that I have chosen to prepare these pages. Let me congratulate you for going through it all the way. It is my sincere hope that you will continue to remain an avid reader of the Scriptures and that you make choices for your eternal destiny.

I want to conclude with this verse of Saint John. 3 John 4 says, *"I have no greater joy than to hear that my children walk in truth."*

So dear reader, what is your position on eternity? Once again, the opportunity is offered to you to ask about what happens after death. If all goes well, great. Otherwise, I urge you to contact the Almighty and ask Him to guide you there. I am confident that you will make the right choice. If, like me, you dream of a better world under the direction of Jehovah, open your heart to Him because He is prepared to enter into it and dwell in it, and give you eternal salvation. May the peace of God which surpasses all understandings be with you and guide you! Thanks!

For comments or more information, contact your local congregation or contact us at:

Jfranc6704@gmail.com

www.successfullife.us

Or mail us a comment:

Jean D. François

P.O. Box 360543

Brooklyn, NY 11236

Biography of The Author

After completing his primary and secondary school studies, Dr. Jean Daniel François studied Administration, Economics, Finance and Theology. He holds a degree in Administration (BS), a license in Theology (Bachelor of Theology), and an MA in Economics (Master of Arts). He also studied medicine at New York Medical College in Valhalla, NY where he earned his doctorate in medicine. He continues his career as a Neurologist in New York where he resides with his wife, Jocelyne, and their two grown up children Jean Daniel and Sarah. Dr. François wrote *Through the Light of Sola Scriptura* from his personal experience, research, readings, and a major concern to help all sincere souls to make an informed choice base on knowledge, the gentle influence of the spirit of God and not on emotions or pressures.

 Reader's Point of View

This book is a useful tool for readers whose occupations preclude biblical study in greater detail. The author of "Through The Light Of *Sola Scriptura*" strives to give a good account of God, the Creator, and his relationship to men. In this 21st Century, the Gospel of Jesus Christ is being replaced by false doctrines and biblical misinterpretations which are very popular in many churches as well as religious television and radio broadcasting programs. In the midst of all this confusion, the author, *Jean Daniel François*, in his deep faith wants to bring that understanding of the 2nd coming of Jesus to others, the way the bible sees it and according to Jesus' instructions. Men must know there is a day of judgment for every vain word they speak or write. It may be of great use to lay down the supreme and sacred principles of which the author was governed by in his writing to explain one thing: to know, love, fear our Lord, and be ready for the 2nd coming of Jesus.

"Behold, I come quickly: hold that fast which thou hast, that no man take thy crown." REVELATION 3:11.

I appreciate the author's effort to proclaim the true Gospel of Jesus Christ, the Lord to humankind. I am hoping readers will appreciate the value of this literary work from the author's pen.

I recommend it highly. This is great reading, indeed!

~ ERNST SAINT-LOUIS, engineer, doctorate candidate in religion, passionate biblical doctrine researcher

Selected Bibliography

If I had to remember or take into account all the books read, the documents consulted, the advice received in writing this book, I am sure I should make another reference book. And even after doing so, I might omit some names. So I resigned myself to write the following names. For others, I appeal to their indulgence! My main source is the BIBLE.

Baron, Will — *Deceived by the New Age*, Pacific Press Publishing Association, Miami, FL 33172

Camping, Harol — *The End of the Church Age … and After*, Family Stations, Inc.

Chadwick, Henry — *The Early Church*, Penguin Books, New York, NY.

Dr. Dobson, James — *When God Doesn't Make Sense*, Tyndale House Publishers, Inc., Wheaton, IL

Finley, Mark — *Satisfied*, Pacific Press Publishing Association, Nampa, ID

Graham, Billy — *Peace With God*, WORD, Incorporated, Waco, TX 76796

Hammer, Dean H. — *The God Gene: How Faith Hardwired Into Our Genes* IS, Doubleday Publishing, September 2004

Maxwell, Arthur S. — *Your Bible and You, (Votre Bible Et Vous)*, Pacific Press Publishing Association, Miami, Fl 33172

Numbers, Ronald L. — *The Creationists*, Random House, 1992, New York.

Sproul, Robert Charles — *The Crucial Questions Series*, Reformation Trust Publishing, Orlando, Fl.

Stanley, Charles F. — *Living The Extraordinary Life*, Thomas Nelson, Inc. Nashville, TN

Swindoll, Charles R. — *Living Above The Level of Mediocrity*, W. Publishing Group, U.S.A.

Weber, Max — *The Protestant Ethic and the Spirit of Capitalism*, Roxbury Publishing Company, Los Angeles, CA 2002

White, Ellen G. — *The Great Controversy*, Harvestime Boooks, Altamont, TN 37301

www.ingramcontent.com/pod-product-compliance
Lightning Source LLC
LaVergne TN
LVHW050633100826
845148LV00011B/1849